HOW TO TAP INTO YOUR OWN GENIUS

by
Thomas Dale Cowan, Ph.D.

Produced by The Miller Press, Inc.

A FIRESIDE BOOK
Published by Simon & Schuster, Inc.
NEW YORK

A Fireside Book
Published by Simon & Schuster, Inc.
Simon & Schuster Building
Rockefeller Center
1230 Avenue of the Americas
New York, New York 10020
FIRESIDE and colophon are registered trademarks of Simon & Schuster, Inc.
Designed by Stanley S. Drate/Folio Graphics Co., Inc.
Manufactured in the United States of America
10 9 8 7 6 5 4 3 2 1

Library of Congress Cataloging in Publication Data

Cowan, Thomas Dale.
  How to tap into your own genius.

  "Produced by the Miller Press, Inc."
  "A Fireside book."
  1. Conduct of life.   I. Title.
BJ1581.2.C68   1984   158'.1   84-13873
ISBN 0-671-53071-2

To my parents

Contents

HOW
TO TAP
INTO
YOUR OWN
GENIUS

1

Listening to Your Genius

To believe your own thought, to believe that what is true for you in your private heart is true for all men—that is genius.

—RALPH WALDO EMERSON

The voice of genius speaks to everyone.

Unfortunately, most people never hear it. Others hear it on occasion, but they distrust and ignore it. And there are some who hear it, follow it, and shape fresh new perspectives about themselves, life, and the universe around them. They use their intuitive insights to live more creatively and successfully in their private pastimes as well as in their careers and professional pursuits. The voice of genius is timeless and has been speaking to people throughout the ages.

Whether you call it intuition, imagination, inspiration, the inner self, the unconscious, psyche, soul, creativity, or genius—it matters very little. The phenomenon has been universally experienced by mankind throughout history. You've experienced it yourself. You've heard it. You've felt it. In a dream, a reverie, while taking out the garbage, jogging, or lying on the beach, often in the most ordinary circumstances, you've had a sudden flash of insight, a direct comprehension of the truth of a situation, a gut feeling, a spontaneous understanding of the how or why of something.

When Robert Frost was asked about his source of inspiration for writing poetry, he replied that it involved "the delight in remembering something I didn't know I knew." Genius is like that. Hearing it is like remembering something we have known all along. In addition to being a personal truth, it also seems to have the ring of universality about it. We know it is true for us and we suspect very deeply that it is true for others as well. Throughout history, scientists, artists, saints, statesmen, military leaders, business people, and individuals in all walks of life have witnessed their genius. It is incorrect to believe that inspiration only transforms poets and mystics because they, better than others, can describe their encounters with genius so poetically or rapturously. Everyone has experienced that inner voice and interior vision at one time or another.

The Human Brain

Since the voice of genius speaks to everyone and it is such a universal experience, why is there so little discussion about it? Why do people not talk more openly about their genius? Are we afraid that others will accuse us of hearing voices? Some people may assume the voice they hear is maladjusted, out of touch with reality, not to be trusted. Other people fear being labeled "crazy" or worry that their friends will think them high-brow visionaries who are no longer fun to be with.

We hesitate to talk about our genius because we have so little scientific data on how genius functions. Like intuition, genius is a mystery: It defies the probings of science, which has never been able to explain it adequately. Brain-research scientists have failed to shed much light on the nature of genius because they concern themselves with cells, neurons, synapses, cortical networks, and chemical and electrical responses on the physical level. Brain researchers study the brain, not the mind. Needless to say, physical studies of the human brain have provided almost no information to illuminate those qualities that are the most strikingly human— memory, consciousness, spirit, belief, faith, love, intuition. In spite of years of research and study, the best researchers and psychologists still know very little about the nature of the human spirit; fortunately, science knows very little about how to control it. Attempts have been made but evidence is sketchy. Proof is almost unattainable and theories conflict.

Perhaps the best evidence science has offered to explain how genius operates is found in split-brain studies. Neurophysiologist Roger Sperry and a few other enlightened mavericks in the scientific community have learned that there is indeed a center in the brain where intuitive activity, hunches, sudden insights, and spontaneous perceptions occur. The right hemisphere of the brain functions intuitively. It deals with images, symbols, and fantasies; it perceives relationships and understands information in holistic terms. Conversely, the left hemisphere operates rationally and analytically, making distinctions, categorizing, and judging. In general, the left side of the brain is dominant in Western thinking. Because our educational system rewards primarily left-brain development in fields like math, language, science, logic, and engineering, this rational mode of thought characterizes the mental activity we use and trust in dealing with everyday reality. Actually, many people with a highly developed left-brain capacity equate reality *only* with data the left side can process. They overlook or distrust the right-brain intuitions. However, following its own brand of logic, the right hemisphere grasps holistic relationships, understands myth and symbol, associates imagery, and penetrates to the essence of things. It also processes information and returns it to us as conscious data, but the means by which it communicates are different from the analytical logic of left-brain activities. Image, insight, hunch, feeling, intuition—these are the right-brain techniques of communication, which we collectively call genius.

Because knowledge of split-brain phenomena has filtered down to so many people in our society, we are entering a new age in which genius and other nonrational modes of understanding are more acceptable. We are no longer immediately labeled mad, schizoid, or incurably romantic if we admit to listening and following our intuitive sources of wisdom. Until recently, however, Western culture was not very receptive to the existence of genius. In fact, the word "genius" is usually reserved only for someone exceptionally talented, creative, smart, or inventive. We are reluctant to apply the term to the population at large, assuming that average men and women do not possess genius—or if they do, it operates on a much lower level than the genius of a Socrates, da Vinci, Michelangelo, Shakespeare, Beethoven, or Einstein. However, a considerable number of professional men and women have undergone various types of personal transformation in the last couple of decades. A new paradigm of reality has emerged for them—a fresh understanding of reality that includes room for the intuitive voice of genius. These "Aquarian Conspirators," as Marilyn Ferguson calls them in her book *The Aquarian Conspiracy,* operate on a higher level of consciousness illuminated by modes of perception that transcend what we have traditionally considered to be reality. They look at the universe and perceive that it functions differently than our Western traditions have suggested.

Still, there are those who do not trust their own genius, let alone anyone else's. Many of these people restrict themselves with the scientific notion that will not accept anything for which we do not yet—nor may ever!—have answers. But skeptics are always with us. Goethe, a recognized genius even in his own time, struggled with the problem of unbelievers two hundred years ago. He berated the narrow minded, narrowly educated individual who, "brought up on the so-called exact sciences, will, from the height of his analytical reason, not easily comprehend that there is also something like an exact imagination." Split-brain research, yoga, meditation, visualization, biofeedback techniques, Zen, dreamwork and trace research, self-hypnosis techniques, ESP, paranormal psychology, and a host of other disciplines have demonstrated conclusively that there is indeed "something like an exact imagination." The visions and voices arising from deep within us have an exactness of their own. They can be trusted when you know how to deal with them. They are as reliable as rational thought, and when paired with rational thought, offer a more holistic perception of the universe.

In fact, Goethe's "so-called exact sciences" have been proven in our own time to be just that—"so-called." The new physics that Fritjof Capra lucidly explains in *The Tao of Physics* is far from exact. The world is so filled with variety, complexity, fluidity, and yet a surprising unity, that even the "hard sciences" are in need of a new language to describe it. Ironically, the scientific descriptions of the natural world have, in recent years, come to sound remarkably similar to the spiritual descriptions of the universe espoused by Eastern mystics. As Capra put it, "The natural world . . . contains no straight lines or completely regular shapes . . . things do not happen in sequences, but all together." It is a "world where . . . even empty space is curved. It is clear that our abstract system of conceptual thinking can never describe or understand this reality completely."

If the best-trained analytical minds, observing the subatomic world, are at a loss for words to describe space, time, energy, and relationships, and their descriptions parallel those of the great mystics of every age, why should we hesitate to relate our own experiences of genius, even though we cannot explain or totally understand them? In dealing with people who consciously and actively exercise their genius, I have found countless men and women who admit an almost total lack of left-brain awareness about their own genius. The left side of the brain cannot fully understand genius because genius speaks another language, the language of myths, symbols, images, and hunches.

You may find much in the following chapters of this book that you will not fully comprehend or understand from a rational, analytical point of view. Even the experts who have spent years training others in meditation, visualization, and other methods of perception do not fully understand precisely why these methods work. But they do work. They unlock energy and power. The possibility lies within each of us to achieve new levels of awareness and other modes of perception.

Levels of Awareness

Genius speaks on several levels.

On the mental level, the voice of genius is most easily recognized by sudden insights in problem solving and decision making. After brainstorming, defining, pondering, or arguing with others, a sudden flash of insight illuminates the solution, and you know instinctively what to do. Often important decisions about a career, marriage, a major move or a change in your lifestyle are accompanied by the voice of genius. In business, it is often called a gut reaction, a shrewd hunch, or a sneaking suspicion. In creative projects, whether writing poetry or devising a mathematical formula, people describe hearing the voice of genius as an "Aha!" or "Eureka!" experience. Suddenly, the poet knows the right word to end a line; the mathematician solves the equation; the scientist realizes the best application for a formula. Often the recognition comes after a period of incubation when you get away from the problem and turn your mind to something else. Incubation. Quiet. Then—flash! An answer!

The answer, solution, or insight often lies outside our usual way of viewing things. Every creative act or idea emerges from a perception in which we feel as if shades have been lifted from our eyes and we can see clearly. Often, mysteriously, the right solution sneaks up when you turn your attention to something else! And no wonder many people refer to their "sneaking" suspicions, since the truth slips in almost unnoticed, creeps up from behind like a friend who covers our eyes and says, "Guess who!" "Who?" "ME!"

The voice of genius also communicates on the emotional level with feelings, vibes, a vague sense that something or someone is either good or bad, favorable or unfavorable, positive or negative. Sometimes the most precise way we can express it is, "It *feels* right (or wrong)." We frequently notice these spontaneous insights in dealing with people or when reflecting on our interpersonal relationships. Many people sense the voice of genius speaking to them when they meet someone for the first time. An intuitive feeling alerts you that you will either like or dislike this new person. At first the feeling is indistinct and undefined. We are troubled or pleased without any clear indication why. As we reflect on it with our rational mind, we begin to perceive reasons for it. We discover if the feeling is valid or invalid.

What most people traditionally mean by "female intuition" is actually just one type of intuition, the kind that operates through feelings and emotions. It is accessible to men as well, and many men heed it as readily and successfully as women. The problem is that in our society men are taught early on to repress and ignore their feelings, whereas women are taught there is nothing wrong with showing emotions. If our culture encouraged boys to express their emotions—to be sensitive to how their genius speaks on the emotional level—we would probably not define intuition as a feminine trait. Nor would we give it second-class status as a mode of knowledge, as so many female attributes have been labeled in a society that values the masculine over the feminine.

The question of whether intuitive feelings can be trusted is exactly the same as whether the rational mind can be trusted. The answer is: Sometimes it can and sometimes it can't. Both can be fooled, and both have the ability to fool us. Often what appears rational and logical turns out to be wrong either for us or for the circumstances, but sometimes it turns out right. The same is true of emotions and feelings. The point is not whether they are one hundred percent correct or not, but that you learn to read them correctly and learn how to treat them against external reality. The intuitive and the rational should be partners, not antagonists. If your past experience has taught you never to trust your feelings, it's probably because you have not discovered what the genius of your emotions is really telling you. The voice of genius speaks through our emotions, but it is possible to hear it clearly and understand it confidently.

Genius also speaks on the physical level, through our bodies and the environment around us. People often hear it when it warns of an impending danger. For example, for apparently no perceivable reason, you suddenly remember you left the stove on or the door unlocked. Without any audible clue, you know someone has walked up behind you. While driving a car, your "motor control" reads the signals of traffic, stoplights, and pedestrians, without your actually paying conscious attention to them. In fact, you may be carrying on a conversation with a passenger, your conscious mind a hundred miles away, not on the road ahead. And yet, when a child darts out in front of you or another car swerves, an inner voice tells your arms and legs how to respond to avoid an accident.

Athletes hear their genius a thousand times a game. If they had to consciously think out every move and play, they would be paralyzed in their tracks. Effortlessly, the good athlete moves, turns, stops, coordinates arms, legs, and eyes without actually thinking about it. The great athletes play intuitively.

Our physical bodies also communicate with us. Illness, disease, stress, the need for exercise—many people hear their bodies cry out for relief before pain actually strikes. It is also possible to read the hidden meanings of pain: pain in the neck, stomachache, dry mouth, shaky knees, sweaty palms, accelerated heartbeat. The mind-body relationship is so intimate that a dialogue is continuously going on between a network of cells, tissues, organs, neurons, synapses, and various control centers in the brain. A psychophysical relationship exists between mind, brain, and body based on information known as biofeedback. Mental and emotional stress harms the body; reciprocally, a weary or undernourished body creates mental and emotional stress.

On the highest level, genius speaks directly to the spirit or soul. Spiritual and mystical intuition is not limited solely to mystics and monks. Average men and women, for no clear reason, when least expecting it, can have an overpowering sense of the Divine. Terms vary for what people perceive as the divine energy or the inexpressible mind behind the universe, but the spiritual experience is usually the same: an incredibly joyous sensation of feeling at one with the universe. We recognize in ourselves a holistic sense of well-being. Things make sense. When trying to describe it, even the most eloquent mystics have been rendered speechless. At best they can relate simply that an inexpressible joy swept over them. They sensed the power or intelligence or harmony of the universe.

On a less religious level, genius can speak to us of other realities than the one in which we spend most of our conscious life. Similar to the knowledge acquired from dreams, drugs, hypnosis, out-of-body experiences, trances, ESP, and visions, mystical intuition makes us aware of other planes of reality. In these moments of revelation, we experience altered states of consciousness in which we hear or see realities that remain hidden from our physical senses in ordinary states. William James said, "Our normal waking consciousness, rational consciousness as we call it, is but one special type of consciousness, whilst all about it, parted from it by the filmiest of screens, there lie potential forms of consciousness entirely different." We can learn methods to hold back those "filmiest of screens." Each of us can discover ways to clarify the divine voice that speaks through our genius.

Learning to Listen

You may have a natural inclination to distrust your genius at first. That we really do possess untapped genius and the ability to rise above our ordinary awareness is awesome. To many, it is frightening. As the psychologist Abraham Maslow suggested, "We enjoy and even thrill to the godlike possibilities we see in ourselves in peak moments. And yet we simultaneously shiver with weakness, awe, and fear before these same possibilities." Unfortunately, many people so distrust their genius that they ignore it, repress it, stifle it, and eventually they learn how not to even hear it.

And yet those very individuals hear their genius when it is uttered by someone else! Our rejected thoughts take on power and truth when others voice the very ideas we heard in our private hearts and thought to be too outlandish to make any sense. If we learned to trust our private heart and not worry about what others think, we would find that our inner voice can be trusted.

If you recognized the truth of this, even though you may be hesitant to admit it, perhaps it is because the preceding pages have expressed your own rejected thoughts. And since you now recognize them as yours, there is an urge to distrust them! Doubts arise; you wonder whether you can really learn how to listen to your genius. The answer is a resounding, "Yes, you can!" It is definitely possible to listen to your genius. Becoming more intuitive, insightful, and creative is not something that depends on IQ, special talents, innate levels of creativity, or advanced courses in education. In fact, our current educational system has a notorious reputation for stifling creativity and intuitive modes of knowledge at a young age. Nature provides us with an inner source of wisdom from which we can extract the truths we need. We would not possess a genius that can and does speak if we were inherently deaf to its voice.

But there is a curious paradox in learning how to listen to your genius. Genius cannot be forced to speak, or to speak louder! But those "filmiest of screens" can be removed. You can learn to foster an attentiveness to genius and discover techniques to create the quiet atmosphere in which you will hear it. Stated in the briefest possible way: *To hear the voice of your own genius you must learn to silence the competing voices.* And the competing voices are everywhere! Some are external noises and environmental distractions that drown out our interior voice. They jam our internal information system and muffle the messages from our psyches. Our work, family responsibilities, daily routines, the clock on the wall, even our material possessions can speak louder than our genius.

Many competing voices are internal. We seem to have an endlessly running dialogue between our social ego and our inner self, a nonstop instant commentary on everything that happens to us. We discuss, complain, suggest, question, insult, plan, regret, and worry over a thousand events and possibilities every day. Mark Twain is reported to have said in his old age that having lived so long he had had many problems, but most of them never happened! Nevertheless, we chatter and worry with ourselves and about ourselves all day long. Our ordinary stream of consciousness, our commonplace routine perceptions, our traditional notion of reality, the usual flow of our thoughts, all these need to be silenced. In terms of the split-brain paradigm, we must learn to "turn off" our left brain sometimes to allow our right brain to communicate with us.

Everyone's genius is a personal entity. Each speaks in

forms and images unique to the individual. It is somewhat similar to dream interpretation. In fact, dreams are a primary mode of communication for most people's genius. There is no standard list of dream symbols that is universally applicable to everyone. When *you* dream about a horse, a banana, an old woman, a lake, or whatever, each is your personal dream symbol. No analyst can truly tell you what they represent; only you can discover their meaning for yourself by studying them over many months or years. Your personal genius also speaks in a private language only you can hear. You must discover it yourself. It means taking a greater responsibility for your interior life. It means accepting a side of your psyche or soul which, as Maslow says, sometimes makes us shiver as we recognize and fear its awesome energies. You may discover that your genius speaks most often on the emotional level. Or you may learn that your genius gives you insights into the creative forces of the universal mind. Some people, on the other hand, find that their genius speaks primarily on the physical or mental levels, solving everyday problems, helping them to make and carry out tough decisions. Each individual is unique and special and has a unique relationship with his or her genius.

Genius and Self-Discovery

It is an exciting adventure to hear your genius—*really* hear it. It can give you a sense of confidence and energy that you may have never experienced before. You can shape your life in accordance with your genius. You may discover that you need not be victimized by the mindless distractions of modern society, nor prey to the deep void so many people find at the core of our culture. Instead, you can construct your own personal paradigm of reality that reflects the world you want to live in, and it will serve as a blueprint for shaping the external events of your life to create that world. We are not innocent bystanders, but participants in reality. By tapping into your own genius, you can improve your daily life and personal relationships. You can discover fresh ideas for successful living at home and at work. You can create your own reality.

Besides enhancing your daily life and stimulating possibilities for creative problem solving and decision making, discovering your genius is a form of self-discovery. Your genius is you. Meeting it, you will acquire greater self-awareness, self-trust, and self-confidence. You will soon realize that your inner voice does speak the truth. Listening to your genius, you'll develop a richer, fuller sense of identity. You'll learn who you really are and always have been.

Tapping into Your Genius

The following chapters are organized according to the competing voices that can stifle your voice of genius. Each deals with one competing voice and shows you strategies to silence it temporarily so that you may listen to your genius. Usually, this means learning how to turn off the left side of the brain temporarily to allow the right side to process and report information in its own distinctive way. When you become reasonably competent at listening to your genius, you must decide whether to follow the advice you hear or not. The secret of living in tune with your genius is not to follow every idea or notion genius puts in your head, but to learn how to interpret each one, evaluate it, and apply it to particular situations. Remember, as a total human being, you have a bicameral brain, and your left hemisphere has some say, too! Intuitive insights need to be refracted through the prism of rational thought. Following your genius does not mean throwing logic, reason, and judgment to the winds to

frolic recklessly and irresponsibly through the fields of imagination and fantasy. We each need to remain a total human
being, composed of both reason and intuition.

It's fair to say that if you have been raised and educated in
the West, you have been overloaded with the value of reason
and logic. You have been taught that clear thinking is rational and logical thinking. Your left brain has little patience
with images, fantasies, dreams, hunches, and intuition. The
exercises that follow are definitely aimed at amplifying the
voice of genius by quieting the voices of reason, disbelief,
certainty, time, routine, and the many voices that speak in the
social roles we all must play in our daily lives. These are the
voices that continuously point out the rational and logical,
the voices that can drown out the voice from our inner heart.

There are important considerations with which you
should approach each topic. Each person is unique. Each has
different needs. Each is at a particular level of self-awareness
already, possessing varying abilities to listen to genius. It is
wise, then, to approach these exercises and strategies realizing that some will be more relevant than others to you. Select
the exercises that most appeal to you, the ones you feel most
comfortable with, those that fit your lifestyle. As a guideline,
focus on those that will strengthen your weaknesses by controlling the competing voices that distract you most.

Keep in mind that the goal of this book is not the exercises themselves. Some of them may not even work for you.
Don't worry; you need not even practice all of them. Your
goal is to acquire a higher level of attentiveness, to learn how
to turn off the distractions of daily life, and listen to your
genius. The exercises are simply the means to help you acquire this attentiveness. They will give you a new attitude,
which you can carry with you into your daily life whether
you continue to practice the strategies or not. You'll find that
the particular exercises and the amount of time you can de-
vote to them will vary as your life changes. You may be able
to incorporate them into your life much like sports, prayer,

or hobbies. At other times, you may be too busy for them. Nevertheless, the attitude they foster, an attitude of attention to your inner voice, can accompany you day after day, no matter how extensive and time-consuming your other activities may be.

Feel free to experiment with the exercises. There is no absolutely right or wrong way to do them. Vary them; let each suggest others. Create your own. This is not a handbook on meditating, visualizing, relaxing, creative problem solving, decision making, or fantasizing—although it includes all these. There are other excellent books dedicated to each of these separate topics, and you can consult them as you go along if you'd like to learn more about them.

Don't become discouraged if the going gets rough. Don't expect to attain nirvana, enlightenment, or initiation as a Jedi warrior immediately. Don't even expect to turn into a so-called "genius." Everyone progresses at his or her own pace. And you will undoubtedly experience what mystics have called "the dark night of the soul" or what we might call "the dark silence of genius." Don't give up—even the nights of silence are periods of growth. The talent to listen to your genius sometimes operates like creative ideas themselves; they need time to incubate. Continue to practice the exercises; experiment with others; have faith. If results are slow in coming, you might find that you are trying too hard.

Remember the curious paradox of genius: to hear it you must be receptive and passive. There's no psychic muscle that will twist the arm of genius and make it speak. For Westerners, the process of letting go, of surrendering to an interior energy over which we have little control, of finding strength by relaxing, all go against our activist grain. Our Promethean personality wants to seize control, steal fire from the gods, and use it to subdue the earth. But as listeners, we must relinquish a certain amount of control. In some ways, we need to follow the Buddhist variation on an old command: "Don't just do something! Stand there!"

When you seem to be getting nowhere, remember that personal transformation does not always happen suddenly or quickly for everyone. It may grow slowly, germinating quietly and unobtrusively like a seed. You are attempting to intuit the true nature of existence as it expresses itself deep within you. In one way or another, almost every society has derived ways to see into the heart of existence, to make sense of the phenomena that surround and bombard the physical senses, to unlock the secret of the universe. Listening to your genius means listening to the voice of the universe as well as the small voice within you.

Be assured that the quest you now undertake has an attainable goal. In fact, the process of self-discovery is self-fulfilling. Your genius is part of you at this moment whether you attend to it or not. You are your genius and your genius is you—just as your mind shares in the repository of the universal mind with access to all of its secrets, mysteries, and truths. Consequently, the truth of your genius must be an integral part of the universal truth. By quieting the competing voices that drown out the voice of genius, you will hear your own genius once again. Even now, before you begin, it speaks to you—making soft suggestions. Do you hear it?

2 | Think Beyond Reason

When the rational mind is silenced, the intuitive mode produces an extraordinary awareness; the environment is experienced in a direct way without the filter of conceptual thinking.

—Fritjof Capra, The Tao of Physics

The voice of reason speaks loud and clear. In fact, clarity is an important aspect of reason. To think clearly is often equated with thinking rationally, having logical reasons to substantiate what you say, showing that your statement has a clearly defined basis in reality. In fact, most communication in society depends upon people speaking clearly and rationally, in order to provide a common ground of understanding from which to speak.

But is the rational mind, the voice of reason, the best voice for communicating with *yourself*? Especially when you're interested in discovering new and deeper aspects of your being? When you want to understand your psyche and unconscious soul—those parts of you that lie beyond reason's grasp—how can they be explained in terms of logic and rationality? They are the intensely felt experiences that you admit are beyond words to describe. They are heartfelt truths too profound for the rational mind to handle.

In many situations, the voice of reason is not the best medium for expressing broader definitions of reality, for enunciating new approaches to practical problems in daily life, the environment, or society. The powers of the rational mind are circumscribed by very limited boundaries. Within these boundaries, the powers of analysis, judgment, evaluation, and logic can often achieve stupendous heights, but those powers must work only within the scope of rational thought. They do not provide new insights or creative ideas; they only catalog, compare, and juxtapose information already acquired. In other words, the rational mind can only recognize and work with what it already contains. It often sounds convincing because it operates on *what it already knows*. But for truly innovative concepts, the voice of reason must remain silent and listen to what genius can discover.

What does it mean to silence the voice of reason?

The voice of reason operates through words and logical sequences. Springing from the left side of the brain, the voice of reason communicates verbally and follows an ordered sequence, a cause-and-effect process that "makes sense." Of course, there's nothing wrong with words or linear sequences, but listening *only* to the voice of reason creates a mental bias about the way we perceive reality. Language shapes our consciousness, and listening primarily to expressions of linear thinking creates the impression that events happen only according to logical cause and effect.

Let's look at words and sequences. Words shape our perceptions. Many people would say it is the other way around—that we have perceptions and then choose the words to describe them. As babies, however, before we have the use of speech or understand it, we have perceptions. A feral child raised alone among wild animals has perceptions, but no words for them unless he creates original words from his natural grunts and groans. Consider also how the choice of words reinforces a perception to the point where eventually the perception persists simply because particular words continue to shape it. Among the various Eskimo peoples there are dozens of words to refer to snow. The subtle distinctions that they see are lost on people who do not live so intimately with snowy conditions. Undoubtedly, if they stopped using certain terms, in time, new generations would fail to see the distinctions. So their choice of words reinforces their perceptions.

Another example of how language shapes consciousness is our discussion of genius. If I limited myself only to speaking of genius as a "spirit dwelling within you," something like the genie in the bottle (another form of the word, by the way!), many readers who don't believe in spirits would never quite understand what I was talking about. However, if I use various words, one will communicate the concept of genius more clearly to you. The illuminating word might be intuition, creativity, inspiration, satori, enlightenment, or insight. So the choice of language has the power to shape our perceptions. Listening primarily to the voice of reason originating from the predominantly verbal left side of the brain can hold us locked into our already established view of the world and ourselves.

Next let's consider the voice of reason's penchant for logical sequences. It may have already occurred to you that a sentence is a line of words in a logical sequence. And what is reasoning? A line of thought that moves from A to B to C. When we reason something out, we try to move logically from the first point to the second, on to the next, and so forth. We create a real "line" of thought. We're usually proud of our ability to do so because it gives us a sense of control. We voluntarily apply the mind (actually only half of our brain) to a problem and "force" an answer. We find causes and effects. We see how things progress, function, and move along. It's wonderful—we are in control!

Creativity researchers, however, have discovered that creative ideas cannot be forced by any line of reasoning. Rather than being under our voluntary control, creative ideas spring from an involuntary mode of receptivity. We do not discover creative ideas by frantically digging through the debris of our conscious data. What is conscious is already known, at this moment, and we find it lacking, inoperative, and unsatisfactory—or else we would not need a new idea. And that's the point. The ideas, solutions, and approaches we already have at our disposal are not adequate or we would not be stumped. Truly creative ideas are not under our control. They are, in a way, independent of us and surface only when we are receptive to them.

When genius speaks on the mental level of problem solving and decision making, it will utter creative ideas on its own. We cannot squeeze or wring them out. We can only be receptive to them. We must assume an attitude of flexibility, which creativity expert Silvano Arieti calls "the ability to abandon old ways of thinking and initiate different directions." Flexibility requires spontaneity on our part to receive what comes spontaneously. Reasoning must move from one point to the next logical point. The voice of genius, on the other hand, produces realizations, skipping middle steps that the voice of reason must plod over before the answer is reached. While reason goes from A to B to C, genius moves from A to D!

It is not easy to silence the voice of reason. It's difficult for us not to view reality in cause-and-effect sequences. In fact, you may wonder what is left if we abandon verbal, linear thought. But verbal thinking is only one aspect of thinking, and thinking itself is only one aspect of consciousness. A great deal of our so-called thinking takes place on an unconscious level that responds and reacts to external events without our really being aware of it. Recall the athlete who does not consciously think out each movement, or the automobile driver who can react to danger automatically. We know we are constantly interacting with external phenomena all the time (even while asleep), much of it on the fringe of our conscious awareness. Now if this type of thinking is on the fringe, where does it take place? How does the mind process these "thoughts" that use no words?

The answer is that we think in terms of images and feelings as well as words. All day, all night, at every moment, we are processing information in the right hemisphere of our brain as images and feelings. Everyone does it unconsciously, without "thinking" about it. Some people have learned to consciously take the time to listen to and understand these inner images, and in the process of working with them, hear the voice of genius. The task before us in this chapter is to learn to think in images and feelings, and to allow the non-verbal mode of thinking to liberate us from the voice of reason. For some people, imaging may not come easily. Our social conditioning has taught us to repress imagery and consider it an inferior mental function akin to daydreaming, fantasizing, and goofing off. The images of daydreams and fantasies are commonly believed to have no basis in external reality and to constitute only an inner reality which is often considered unimportant. Yet, in terms of listening to our genius, this inner reality is as important as external reality—and sometimes more so.

Let's start listening to genius by silencing the voice of reason. We will begin to think in feelings, images, and other nonlinear elements. It's the vital first step in discovering how the world of genius operates.

Imaging

Everyone has the capacity to produce images in the mind that, to a greater or lesser degree, replace conceptual thought. Some people can image better than others. Artists, writers, designers, and engineers, for example, are trained to "see" with their mind's eye what they intend to produce.

Being able to work with images is an important process in creativity. If we have repressed images for whatever negative bias we have held against them, we have also repressed our capacity for imaging. But, fortunately, imaging is a common right-brain activity that can be improved with practice. Different people use images for different purposes, but our goal is to produce images in order to reverse a trend that has prevented us from hearing the interior voice of our genius. We want to temper our attachment to abstractions and conceptual ideas.

Athletic coaches frequently have their athletes envision their performance before an upcoming event. Quite the opposite from watching the tapes in reruns after the game! Instead, a football player might envision himself receiving a pass—turning his head, spotting the ball in the air, feeling his arms and hands go up, feeling the ball hit his palms, noticing how his legs keep moving, watching other players out of the corners of his eyes, and so forth. Bruce Jenner kept a hurdle in his living room while training for the Olympics for this same purpose. He said it wasn't there just for inspiration, but so that he could imagine himself running up to it and leaping over it.

Let's try a visualization exercise.

EXERCISE:

The Mind's Eye

All visualization experts agree that to get ready to visualize, you must get comfortable, relax, be alone or create a psychic solitude around you. Take deep breaths, allowing your breathing to become rhythmical. There are numerous books on relaxation techniques, breathing exercises, and meditation and visualization methods. If you feel you need more instruction, find a book that appeals to you and practice. But for now, just relax, get comfortable, and breathe deeply and naturally in your own way.

Next, visualize some athletic activity in which you regularly engage, or picture yourself dancing with your favorite dancing partner, or simply performing some daily physical activity which you seldom think about consciously. Try to see yourself doing it. Don't worry if you don't "see" anything at first. Gradually, you'll produce images. You might discover that you are like an observer watching yourself, actually seeing yourself moving through the actions. Some people, however, don't see themselves, but they "feel" themselves moving through all the motions of their imagined activity. Both techniques are fine. The important thing is to bring the scenes into your consciousness and recreate all the kinesthetic feelings that go with them. Also try to visualize other sensations: sounds, smells, temperatures, tactile impressions. Stir up all the sense impressions that are associated with your activity.

The important point is not to name them. Naming is not visualizing. Your left brain will not like this activity for two reasons: It takes too long and the left hemisphere doesn't deal easily with images. It'll tell you, "Look, name all those sensory impressions and get it over with!" Don't pay attention to it. This is an exercise in which you are *seeing* things, not *thinking about words*. So don't say the word "sweaty" to yourself. Imagine instead how sweat feels running down your body. Don't say "whirling" and let it go at that. Experience in your mind's eye the sensation of whirling around.

Continue this exercise for at least five or ten minutes. Allow yourself to become mesmerized by it. The right side of your brain will love it.

There are some variations on this basic visualizing exercise. Image a scene with which you are familiar: a street, a beach, the interior of a room. Don't worry if you can't see all the sights, sounds, smells, and tastes at one time. Be content with the ones you can re-create for yourself.

After you have done that, visualize a scene where you have

never been before. Literally create a new place in your mind's eye.

Several things happen when you do this exercise. You are reversing your tendency to abstraction by giving your thoughts concrete form, shape, and texture. Events and phenomena stored in the mind tend to become abstractions that are cut off from you. They become dim memories, disembodied concepts that lose their rich, sensuous nature—color, weight, shape, size, and smell. But sensory thinking, or visualization, bridges the inner self with the outer world, bypassing the voice of reason. And this is important. Genius, by expressing itself in things and feelings rather than abstract concepts, creates a reproduction of the external world inside you, on the sharp screen of your imagination where verbal thought is unnecessary. Genius reminds you that the physical body—the part of you that plays racqetball or cooks dinner—is not an abstract concept merely to be thought about after the fact, but a subject that can re-experience those activities in very much the same way—with all their sensory richness—whenever it wants to. The schism between the I and the me is created by the voice of reason saying, "Look, you're not dancing now, you're not making pizza now. That you is another you that isn't here right now." But genius disagrees—*that* you is here right now, stored in consciousness as textural memories and sensations of your physical body. It is still part of you.

The Proper Symbol

Ralph Waldo Emerson believed that if a person wishes to express an idea without losing any of its impact in the process of communication, the thought behind the idea must be connected with its "proper symbol." Visualization is the first step toward thinking in symbols and metaphors that will stand as solid reconstructions for abstract ideas. To connect your thought with its proper symbol is a major breakthrough in listening to your genius because genius speaks with symbols and metaphors. As Einstein put it, "A thought comes, and I may try to express it in words afterwards."

Well, how did the eminent scientist handle the thought prior to finding the words for it? By image and metaphor. In 1907, he had the image of a person falling off a roof and watching another object fall with him. It suddenly occurred to Einstein that the person falling would think the law of gravity had vanished, because the object would be accelerating at the same rate as he was. Calling this notion that occurred first in imagery "the happiest thought of my life," he went on later to develop it into his theory of gravity and relativity.

You already connect some thoughts with metaphors. When you say, "It's hotter than hell" rather than "It's exactly 110 degrees in the shade," you have spoken metaphorically. When your friend "skunks" you at cards and you reply, "You rat!" you are using metaphors. We say that so-and-so is "foxy." Someone else is "sharp as a whip." Expressing ourselves with things rather than concepts is a normal pattern of speech. What we now want to do is get better at it, use metaphors consciously, and eventually fall into the habit of using them whenever we can to replace our left-brain abstractions.

By creating euphemistic abstractions, we strip many events of their rightful images. After World War II, for instance, we renamed the War Department the Defense Department because of the more positive connotation of defense. Nevertheless, it is the Defense Department that wages war. During the Vietnam War era, "body count" replaced "dead soldiers," and "fire power" replaced the terms that would have conjured up real images of guns, tanks, and other weapons. "First-strike capability" totally ignores the moral point of "starting a war."

EXERCISE:

The Proper Symbol

Images won't hold still, but they aren't supposed to—they have a life of their own. To become familiar with metaphors and to experience how they can vary, enriching one idea after another, try the following exercise. Choose an image—a concrete, physical thing, such as a face. Then list as many metaphors using that image as you can: face of danger, face of a cliff, face of a clock, face-off. Or, for example, eye: eye of a hurricane, eye of a potato, eye of a needle.

Choose an image that has not already been loaded with clichés. For example, cloud: cloud of anger, cloud of ideas, cloud of distractions, cloud of mistrust, cloud of happiness. There are no right or wrong metaphors in this exercise. The point is to watch how your right brain suggests images that you've never put together with your symbol before.

Play with these images for a while, then let your left brain analyze them to see if they have something in common. Do they all fit into some general category? When I worked with "cloud," the metaphors that occurred first and most easily were ones that implied confusion or disruption. Most likely at the time I did it, the image of cloud suggested "clouding up," as in obscuring, fogging, blocking from view. I had to force "cloud of happiness." Its meaning was not immediately clear. Perhaps the image of cloud switched from "fogging up" to "floating." Now I have a different, pleasant set of associations: cloud of joy, cloud of good health, and so on.

Experiment with other images, or put Emerson's advice to work and think of some statement you would like to make, then sift around for the proper symbol or image for it.

When working with symbols, don't be alarmed if the metaphors you construct appear to distort or deform reality. The voice of reason may scold you for it, but remember that reason is uncomfortable working with images and concepts that it is not familiar with. We must be liberated from meticulously reproducing what reason already knows. The first whispers of creativity come from genius, which may show us a slightly skewed version of reality out of which arise the creative alternatives we seek.

Visualizing and using concrete metaphors come naturally to us, even though we have been trained to think that such practices exaggerate and mislead. Memorize the words below in column A until you can recite them in order without looking at them. Then memorize the words in column B.

A	B
concept	house
integrity	rainbow
utilization	nurse
statement	table
type	garbage
distraction	railroad track
synthesis	basement
gain	mountain
reference	cathedral
disability	tomato

You probably discovered that it was much easier to memorize column B. The words in column A are abstract nouns with very little sensory content—no visual, aural, tactile, or kinesthetic clues. The nouns in column B, however, are rich in concrete associations. You can see, hear, feel, and smell them. They are much easier to memorize.

EXERCISE:

Deepening a Metaphor

Choose a metaphor for some situation. Let's say you just had a business meeting and you came away thinking, "How slimy!" *Slimy* is a good metaphor. Now deepen it by adding new associations: What color is slimy? What temperature? What animals are slimy? What plants? Which of the four elements (earth, air, fire, water) make up slimy? Where is slimy? Is slimy young or old? And so on.

Choose your own metaphor and add to it until it becomes rich with connotations and nuances. When you think you've exhausted them, try their opposites. Create a deeper metaphor for the opposite image of your choice.

This exercise is very useful in many daily situations when you want to reflect on what has happened to you in a nonrational, right-brain manner. For example, when your teenager has just infuriated you for the hundredth time this week, when your co-worker at the office continues to aggravate you with some annoying habit, or when you're trying to decide how best to spend the extra money you saved last month, don't just mull over the situation, thinking up reasons pro and con about how you should handle it. Instead, let a metaphor pop into your consciousness and then spend several minutes deepening it with other associations. As it expands and offers insights that reason would never have suggested, you may discover positive aspects about your teenage child, or notice the humorous side of the office predicament, or even realize better ways to spend your money. You'll be surprised by the insights metaphorical thinking will give you that purely rational reflection ignores. Not only will you discover new dimensions to the event, but you'll discover other sides of your response to it, that is, other sides of yourself.

Keeping a Journal

It is a good idea to keep a journal as you learn to listen to your genius, recording exercises when it seems appropriate or just keeping track of your day-by-day progress. You may want to keep a record of insights, discoveries, and revelations. A journal is a recognized tool for self-discovery and self-awareness. Many therapists recommend it; artists, scientists, and other creative people find it indispensable for their work. It is the perfect process for uniting the left and right hemispheres of the brain in a single activity. The use of words will appeal to your left brain (although you might want to sketch or draw in your journal, too). And the right brain enjoys the reflective, quiet, meditative process of keeping a journal. It triggers associations and memories and images that would never come to consciousness were it not for the fact that you are recording your experiences on paper.

EXERCISE:

The Single Metaphor

On a trip through the Himalayas, the author Peter Matthiessen experienced a moment of joyous enlightenment which he wanted to record in his journal. Words failed him and the only image he could think of that captured the experience was "Smile." So he recorded that one word, and it was enough.

Try doing the same for your daily experiences. Keeping a journal does not have to be an arduous task of composing lengthy paragraphs. Entries can be quite brief. Even after writing at great length about a specific experience, sum it up with one pure image. Choose something physical, not an abstraction. Avoid words like sad, happy, joyful, and frustrated. Choose clear-cut nouns and verbs: tears, laugh, sunlight, lift, ocean, soar, mud. Make your single metaphor a thing or an action.

Feelings as a Way of Knowledge

We have believed that "thinking" is "knowing" for so long that we have become oblivious to other ways of knowing, including a major one: feeling. Put very simply, emotions provide knowledge. It is not just the things that we can *think* about that we *know*. We can know things without thinking about them. Affective cognition takes place every day in each of us. For example, every time you discover you are right about something, you experience the "joy of verification." It's a delightful exuberance that sweeps over you when you prove that something you had predicted actually turned out to be true. The intensity of the joy is related to how important the prediction or problem is. It is similar to the joy of solving a problem. Another common emotional response that accompanies knowledge is surprise. You experience surprise when things do *not* occur as you had expected. When "taken by surprise," you experience something for which you were unprepared. Some surprises are pleasant, some are not.

EXERCISE:

A Record of Unexpressed Emotions

Events that elicit the "joy of verification" or surprise at the unexpected are quite common, yet we seldom allow our emotional selves to fully engage in those events. Each of us has weekly, maybe daily, experiences in which we repress the emotional responses. We don't allow our total being to learn from the experience because we squelch the emotional part of ourselves for reasons which may or may not be justified. For example, your boss criticizes you for mistakes in a report that were not your fault. You know that she won't accept your excuses. You feel like getting angry and blaming some associate who was really at fault—but you don't. You keep your mouth shut and never express those emotions. You may carry them home with you and kick the cat or take them out on your spouse or children. Not every emotion can be expressed immediately, and frequently those unexpressed emotions are directed toward unsuspecting people who don't deserve them. The same is true of positive emotions. Sometimes we can't express love or gratitude or joy because it would be "out of place" or we would be taking advantage of a situation or we might embarrass the recipient of our affection. So we say nothing.

If we were to express or accept our emotions in the situations that elicited them, we would understand those situations more fully. We would get deeper insights into the circumstances themselves, into ourselves, and into the way people react to us.

How often do you not express your emotions?

Keep a record of your unexpressed emotions organized by days of the week. Divide each day into morning, afternoon, and evening. Record: 1) the emotional event, 2) how you felt, 3) what you said, and 4) what you did not say or would like to have said. At the end of the week, notice how many of your emotions are unexpressed. Do you live a life in which major emotions are stifled? Or is the basic thrust of your life to learn from events by actively experiencing and expressing the emotions that accompany those events?

If you're still not sure how the emotions are pathways to knowledge, try the following strategy. It's really something you do automatically, but by making an exercise out of it, you will consciously see how you learn about something through your affective response.

EXERCISE:
_____

Clicking Your Emotional Shutter

The perfect tool for this exercise is one of those large, expensive, glossy books found in the photography sections of bookstores, one with numerous photos on a variety of subjects. A magazine with plenty of photos will also work. My preference is for photos of landscapes or people at work, but faces will suffice, too. Be sure the photos you use do not have any words on them. It's best not to use photos in magazine ads; not only are there boldly lettered words telling you what you should feel, but the advertising photo itself is a premeditated effort to elicit a particular emotional response from you.

To get ready, sit down, breathe deeply, relax, and close your eyes for a few moments with the book of photos on your lap. Choose a quiet place where you won't be distracted by outside noises, preferably a place where there is not a lot of movement or activity.

Open to a photo, look at it for a second or two, then close your eyes, imagining that your eye is the shutter of the camera. What is the first emotion that you recognize? What is the feeling you just caught on the film of your psyche? Happiness? Peace? Turmoil? Sorrow? After you've isolated the emotion, experience it for a minute. Then open to the photo and look at it, noticing its various parts, discovering which facets elicited your particular emotion. Was the emotion justified? Do you feel like changing your feeling (not mind!) about it? Why?

Next use imaginative visualization to create the events that surround the moment captured on film. How did those people get there? What are their personalities like? What did they do in the next minutes *after* the photo was taken?

Repeat this with as many photos as you like. The point is to experience how your right brain, reacting immediately to visual stimulation, triggers certain emotional responses. During these exercises, the left brain is put on hold until you look at the picture steadily, analyzing its components to determine why you had the emotional response you did. But it really doesn't matter why in the long run. The response itself is the goal. What you are experiencing is your right brain giving you a gut-level feeling about a scene, a face, or a situation.

The notion of learning and knowing on a nonverbal level may be hard to grasp at first. We have long assumed that all knowing and all cognition must involve words and ideas. But where is the "place of knowing"? Is it the brain? Is it only the brain? Ironically, "knowing" as a function of the brain has been "known" for only the last 500 years. Ancient peoples placed the seat of intelligence in various parts of the body. The very early Greeks, for instance, did not have a single word for consciousness. Rather they employed a host of terms for what is known to us as consciousness. Most often used were words for lungs, breath, heart, gut, belly. Expressions that persist even today such as "I feel it in my bones," "My gut reaction is to . . . ," "The thought of doing that takes my breath away" indicate that the vestiges of this era remain.

We do sense stimuli with other parts of the body and process that information in unconscious areas of the psyche. What we feel in our gut, heart, belly, bones, or skin is real knowledge transmitted along neural linkings that eventually becomes part of our understanding.

An interesting experiment was performed with subjects who were told that their heartbeats would be monitored so that they could hear them while being shown pictures of different scenes. The subjects were to rate each picture on an interest scale, from "not very interesting" to "very interesting." It has been established that when we are interested in something our heartbeat increases, and it slows down when we are disinterested. Unknown to the subjects of this experiment was that they were listening to other people's heartbeats, not their own. The results of the experiment were, in the words of Barbara B. Brown, experiential physiologist and student of mind-body phenomena, "surprising," "frightening," and "disturbing." Subjects rated the pictures according to the fake heartbeats! A slow phony heartbeat rated the picture uninteresting, a fast heartbeat won a higher interest rating. Even weeks later when the subjects were told about the "set up" and asked to rate the pictures again, they held to their original judgments! What is truly disconcerting is that the subjects indicated their level of interest according to the rate of the faked heartbeat! Even when a subject's actual heartbeat slowed down, indicating a lower level of interest in a photo, the subject rated the photo of high interest if it was accompanied by someone else's accelerated heartbeat.

It seems clear that in some circumstances, external and conscious stimuli or messages can drown out internal, unconscious messages from parts of the body to the mind. There may be situations in which the body is literally trying to tell us something, but because of some external distraction or deliberate jamming, we fail to hear it on the unconscious level. Or if we do hear it, we fail to allow the unconscious to speak to us. In effect, we jam the voice of our own genius.

EXERCISE:

Body Knowledge

List all the common expressions that refer to a condition of the body and that indicate a message about your emotional or mental state (e.g., "trembling hands" "sick to my stomach," "pain in the neck," "dry mouth," "weak knees," "spineless," etc.) Write down next to each condition the emotional or mental state that each suggests.

Now list parts of the body for which you can create your own representative images. For example, the sole of the foot—is it something akin to being "down at the heels"? Is the elbow somehow related to "impatience," such as in "elbowing your way through a crowd"?

Then try it in reverse. List emotional or mental states and let them suggest to you a part of the body through which they might be expressed. Joy, tranquility, surprise, fear—where are these located in your body?

The next time you are in a situation that elicits an emotional response, such as boredom, enthusiasm, curiosity, or lethargy, find the spot on your body where that emotion expresses itself. The goal of this exercise is to become more conscious of the relationship between our minds and bodies, and to think of psychological states in concrete terms—i.e., as parts of the body.

Many of our bodily messages are not detectable on a conscious level. The average person is completely unaware of them as they produce their effects somewhere deep in the psyche, unless they are being jammed as in the case of the phony heartbeats! Consciousness is not necessary for all forms of learning. The following is a little experiment you can do to test this. Take two similar objects that are of slightly unequal weight, such as pencils, pens, rocks, or mugs of unequal amounts of water. With your eyes half closed, pick each one up and judge which is heavier. Watch yourself do this; concentrate on what is actually going through your mind. What are you becoming aware of? Which clues are telling you the weight of the objects? Feel the objects against your skin, in the palm of your hand; notice the pull of gravity. Then make your decision. The curious factor is that you won't know exactly why or how or when the decision was made. "Something" told you without words, even without clearly identifiable evidence. In other words, the process of judging is not totally conscious. It is the result of physical sensations, information running along the nervous system, rather than of "conscious" thought.

EXERCISE:

Pet Rock

Listening to your genius involves becoming adept at picking up and reading nonconscious signals transmitted through your nervous system to areas of the brain where those signals can be deciphered into awareness. To acquire this skill, let me introduce you to a new friend—a rock. (Or use a stick or leaf or any natural object you've never touched before.) Go outside and pick up a rock or stick. Immediately close your eyes, sit down, and feel it. Notice how heavy it is, where it protrudes, where it is sharp or smooth, where it has corners, feels dry or wet, cold or warm. Visualize the lines and cracks in it, where it is spotted or stained. Spend ten or fifteen minutes getting to know this rock without looking at it.

Then treat your rock as a person. Ask it how old it is, what its name is if it has a name, where it came from, what its personality is like. Ask it why it picked you. (You were attracted to each other, weren't you?)

As you do this exercise, look into yourself as well, to discover why and how you are acquiring this information about your rock. What physical clues are you reading? What interior voice is telling you things about your rock?

If you felt silly pawing over a simple rock, it's probably because it seemed like a childish activity. It was. Children treat rocks and natural objects that way, closely observing them, staring at them until their eyes go out of focus, giving them names, treating them like special friends. It seems to be a natural human activity to want to experience the natural world on intimate terms, even terms of equality. (Why *did* that particular rock choose you?) Adults are not supposed to do those things, and your left brain undoubtedly thought the whole experience was foolish and a waste of time. But as you will see in the next chapter, one of the competing voices is the voice of adulthood, and you'll need strategies such as this one to hush it up on occasion when the voice of genius wants to speak.

Block That Line of Thought!

When someone can't follow your line of thought, they may accuse you of "talking in circles." People who think in images may claim you're "beating around the bush." However they express it, don't be offended. For our purposes, it's good to talk in circles now and then to silence the voice of reason, which prefers linear talking. The sequential reasoning process, where one idea logically follows another, is used every day and, in truth, explains how much of the world operates. To a great extent, it is reliable, predictable, and understandable. Linear or verbal thinking, however, creates the impression that reality is limited to cause and effect phenomena. Now what we know about genius is that it frequently leaps over many intervening steps in the logical process. It darts like a spirit or elf from one notion to the next, often without any logical motivation. We do ourselves wrong and cheat the wisdom of genius when we limit ourselves to linear thinking. It is like forcing ourselves to walk down the middle of the street, never allowing ourselves to wander, to peek in store windows or explore what's happening on the sidewalk and in yards. Every researcher who has studied the creative process has attested to the need to deviate from set assumptions and the usual way of approaching problems. In other words, we need to wander—physically, mentally, and emotionally.

EXERCISE:

Hurricane Thinking

What some creativity experts call "mind maps" I like to think of as "hurricane thinking." What is hurricane thinking? Let me tell you what it's not. Suppose you had to give a talk or write a paper on Cape Cod. The left-brain, linear approach would be to decide what you want to say first, then expand on that. Next determine the logical point that would come from your first statement and develop that. Have a beginning, middle, and end. In general, proceed from one point to the next until you've reached the last thing you want to say. You would probably even outline this on a piece of paper, starting at the top of the page and working down, putting subsections slightly indented under major headings, and so forth. That's not hurricane thinking.

To organize a talk on Cape Cod using hurricane thinking, write "Cape Cod" in the middle of a piece of paper and circle it. The main topic is the eye of your hurricane. Then write whatever ideas occur in whatever order somewhere around it. If a related idea springs from another, write it close to its parent idea and draw a line to it. Then, if a completely unrelated association springs to mind, write it on the opposite side or corner of the page and let it produce its own associated ideas. Continue this process until the page is filled with minor points swirling around the calm eye of Cape Cod in the middle of the page. What you might end up with is something like the example on page 49.

The important point in this exercise is not to evaluate any idea. Nor should you decide which topics are more important than others at this stage. If they are all related to the eye of your hurricane, put them down. Just let your brainstorming produce as many ideas as possible. Then if you really need to organize your clusters of images and ideas for a formal presentation to someone who doesn't want to walk into your hurricane, you might try linking them up or circling them with different colored pencils to see

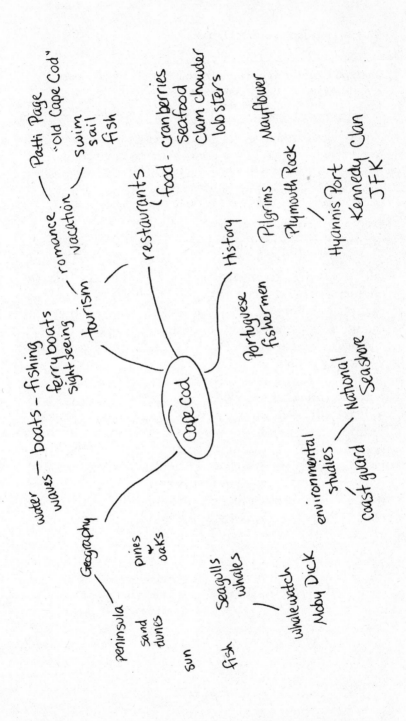

Cape Cod

Geography
- peninsula
- sand dunes
- sun
- pines → oaks
- Fish — Seagulls, whales
- water — boats — fishing — ferryboats
  - sightseeing
- whalewatch — Moby Dick
- environmental studies — coast guard — National Seashore

Tourism
- water — boats — fishing
- ferryboats
- sightseeing
- romance — Patti Page — "Old Cape Cod"
  - vacation — swim, sail, fish
- restaurants — food — cranberries, seafood, Clam chowder, lobsters

History
- Portuguese fishermen
- Pilgrims — Mayflower
- Plymouth Rock
- Hyannis Port — Kennedy Clan — JFK

which go logically with which, or what sequence seems most appropriate for a formal presentation.

Hurricane thinking is a good exercise for observing your mind at work when it isn't constrained by any preconceived pattern of how to arrange thoughts. It is also an excellent tool for coming up with as many ideas, images, and associations as possible before you start your writing. You may eventually conclude that some of the ideas are not appropriate, but that's okay. These can be discarded, or they might serve as the nuclei for other creative projects. Notice how you went around in circles, jumping from one idea to another, expanding on a particular topic for a moment, then dropping it as another occurred to you. The voice of genius can speak on many topics at once and lead you down strange and unexplored avenues of thought, often showing you ideas you forgot you knew.

If you are like most people, every time you engage in hurricane thinking, you will be surprised by ideas that seem to leap forth from your memory or unconscious. Truth tends to leap out at us when we are least expecting it. It simply skips the ordinary reasoning process and rises to awareness, takes its bow, and expects to be applauded. But you don't have to sit around waiting for truth to make its grand entrance. There are tricks that people have used for centuries to coax truth to come forward, to jolt it into consciousness.

EXERCISE:

Spontaneous Divination

If the word "divination" sounds archaic and mysterious, it is. But the psyche is also archaic and mysterious. We're on solid ground even though that ground may be where spirits and oracles once trod. What is divination and how is it spontaneous?

To explain in terms that your rational left brain will understand, spontaneous divination refers to various techniques to startle your unconscious into producing ideas or concepts that are just below the threshold of consciousness. Free association is a form of spontaneous divination. For example, most people, when asked to say the word that comes immediately to mind when they hear the word "father," will say "mother." "Table" . . . "chair." There are some rather predictable and normal associations. In the minutes prior to hearing the triggering word, you were not consciously thinking of your mother or a chair. What happens is that one idea can jolt a related idea out of the unconscious.

We want to jolt unpredictable associations out of the unconscious. Let's say you're stumped on a problem you're trying to solve at work or a family situation that's worrying you. You need new and fresh ideas. Spontaneous divination is a method to trigger fresh ideas. There are several ways to do it. Simply open a book at random, such as a dictionary, a Bible, Shakespeare, or a book of poetry. Then run your finger down the page with your eyes closed. Pause on any given line, open your eyes, and read it. Whatever line you pick becomes the oracle to help solve your problem or get you over your block.

Let's say you're trying to decide how to tell your parents that you're moving out of town, and you've exhausted all the reasons. You need better ones. So you close your eyes, open the Bible, run a finger down the page, open your eyes, and read it. "The Lord will tend the fruitful vines." Then use the images and advice of this sentence to suggest solutions to the problem. You might even do a little hurricane thinking about the words "Lord," "tend," "fruit-ful," and "vines." Or simply ask yourself: How do the images in this sentence (or phrase or word) relate to my problem? In this case, you might be reminded to tell your parents that you must "tend" to your career and for this you need to move. You need to pull up "roots" here and put down new roots elsewhere. You might suggest that your relationship with your parents is indeed "fruitful" and will continue to produce good things no matter how many miles away you are. Sometimes the associations will indeed flash out before you; sometimes nothing will happen. If so, close the book and try another passage.

Another method is to look out the window and let the first object or situation you see be your omen. It might be a passing blue Chevrolet, a flock of birds flying overhead, a child chasing a ball, or an approaching thunder cloud. Whatever it is, assume that the universe has just presented you with a source of possible ideas for your problem and let your genius go at it. Ask yourself: How is what I have just seen related to my problem? You'll be surprised how often the voice of genius will speak to your problem through the images you see out the window.

If you doubt that random events can unlock your uncon-scious feelings about things because there seems to be no cause-and-effect principle operating, the next time you are undecided about what course of action to take, try flipping a coin. Not to find out what to do, but how you feel about your decisions. Heads you will, tails you won't. When the coin comes down, if your gut reaction is, "Oh, no . . . damn!" then you know you don't really feel good about that option. You might still decide on it for very valid reasons, but the simple toss of the coin will immediately release your uncon-scious feelings about that course of action. If, on the other hand, you look at the tossed coin and think, "Whew . . . good!" then you know that your heart truly lies with that choice. You might decide that for legitimate reasons you will have to deny your heart this time and take the other course of action, but you'll have discovered what your genius really feels about the matter.

Synchronicity

Carl Jung proposed a term for certain coincidences that seem to have a special meaning, for which there is no apparent cause and effect. He called this principle synchronicity. In spontaneous divination, a person is acting on the belief that there are certain patterns of chance, certain configurations of people, places, words, events, images, occurrences, which contain some significant meaning. A synchronicity is usually considered to be an unplanned coincidence in which you become an active participant because the events unlock some meaning in your unconscious. To others they are simply coincidence. To you they have meaning. Your genius ferrets out the meaning or recognizes it spontaneously.

Once on a weekend retreat, a group of twelve of us were sitting on a grassy meadow in upstate New York doing the pet rock exercise. In this exercise, however, we sat in a circle, and a rock was given to each of us with our eyes closed and taken away after ten or fifteen minutes before we could look at it. All the rocks were then placed in the center of our ring, and each of us had to go up and recognize his or her rock. Mine had been an extremely small, pebble-size rock, and because of its size I figured I would have no trouble spotting it. The problem was that a second small rock of the same shape and texture was placed immediately next to it. Not knowing which of the two was mine from where I sat, I silently said to the rock (I felt I had gotten to know it fairly well in the fifteen minutes we sat together on the grass!), "Which one are you?" I leaned forward to see more clearly, and immediately a tiny ant crawled up onto the larger stone where the two small red pebbles sat, circled around the one on the left and crawled back down off the larger stone. I knew instantly that the one on the left was mine. The universe had responded! It gave me a sign! A synchronicity that had meaning only for me. I waited anxiously because there was still the chance that someone in our circle (we were taking turns in retrieving our personal rocks) would take mine. But just as the thought crossed my mind, a woman on the other side of the circle crawled to the center, paused, looked at both small red stones for what seemed to me an eternity, then took the one on the right and went back to her place, leaving the rock selected by the ant for me.

Occurrences like this happen more frequently than we realize, but to spot them and appreciate them, a person must be attuned to his or her inner subjective states of consciousness and be able to intuitively link them to external events that are related by meaning. An inner thought, vision, dream, need, or feeling elicits a response from the universe, suggesting that the outer world and one's private interior world are not just *apparently* conjoined but *actually* linked through meaning, metaphor, and myth.

Many people commonly experience synchronicities when they have been worrying anxiously about a relative or friend, wondering if they are all right. And then, out of the blue, the relative or friend calls on the phone! Again, an inner need—to know about a loved one—and an outer event that seems to respond to your inner need.

In order to spot synchronicities one needs an ability to work with images and metaphors, to notice patterns, to appreciate the underlying unity of the universe that Eastern mystics and now Western physicists keep calling to our attention. We need to believe that the outer world really does reflect our interior world, not just that it seems to. In general, Western minds are not trained to perceive these underlying unities, these co-incidences that bridge the illusory gulf between external and internal reality and demonstrate that the universe around us does respond and even corresponds to the universe in our psyches. Genius has the ability to see and point out to us these correspondences, but to hear our genius we need the ability to visualize, recognize inner feelings, and experience life metaphorically. Then we will hear genius speak of the synchronistic world in which we live. It is a comforting realization to see that "we are not alone" but living in a matrix of meaning and purpose, where outside objects and events understand our interior thoughts and needs just as we can understand external objects and events.

EXERCISE:

Getting in Sync with the Universe

Just as some people never remember their dreams until they read a book on dreams or hear a lecture or go to a dream workshop and then start dreaming and remembering them every night, many people conclude they never have synchronicities simply because they haven't taken them seriously or trained themselves to watch for them. Then once they start, synchronicities occur more frequently. Many students of consciousness believe that synchronicities occur very frequently, but because we are too busy with other things and we don't watch for them, they pass us by.

To improve your ability to spot synchronicities, start keeping track of them in your journal. At the end of each day review the day's events for synchronicities, the ones that leap out at you and the ones you may have overlooked. Not every synchronicity is as dramatic as an ant crawling over a rock! Scan the day's events for unusual occurrences or unexpected happenings, things that took you by surprise, moments of chance or coincidence, and spend a few moments attempting to divine the meaning of them. Many times nothing will come of it. Don't fake it—synchronicities can't be made up! Your genius will tell you when you're stretching it, and soon you'll grow confident that you can tell the real ones from the wishful-thinking ones.

The purpose of tuning out the voice of reason temporarily is not to abandon rational thought, verbal skills, logical reasoning, and the obvious cause and effect principle that lies behind so many phenomena. It's taken us centuries to learn all this, and we shouldn't toss it out the window. But the voice of reason must keep silent now and then to allow its partner, the voice of genius, to speak. If the exercises in this chapter have been successful for you, you have now experienced what it is like to view the world and your daily experiences from a nonrational, nonlinear perspective. With practice, hearing the voice of genius comment on your daily activities will become second nature to you. It should, after all, because it is part of your nature to hear it. But the term "second nature" is itself misleading! It suggests that to think in images, to perceive the metaphorical truth of being, to visualize different realities, or to feel your way toward knowledge is somehow "second best" or in fact a "second" nature, something to be applied to your first and original nature. Yet such is not the case.

As mystics and creative people have attested throughout history, this mode of perception is our original nature. It most likely accounted for the earliest conscious experiences of human beings, far back on the ladder of evolution. Simply because we have progressed beyond that point is no reason to assume that those primal skills are gone forever, or that they are useless. In many of us they merely lie dormant. For artists, mystics, poets, visionaries, and creative people in every field, they are far from dormant. They are alive, vibrant, revolutionary. As we tap into the energy of our genius, we develop the power to see, hear, think, and feel in that original way.

3

Return to Childhood

Every child begins the world again, to some extent, and loves to stay outdoors, even in wet and cold. It plays house, as well as horse, having an instinct for it. Who does not remember the interest with which when young he looked at shelving rocks, or any approach to a cave? It was the natural yearning of that portion of our most primitive ancestor which still survived in us.

—HENRY DAVID THOREAU

The "natural yearning" of our most primitive ancestor is still a part of our original nature. It is the part in us where we, like those ancestors, can hear the voice of genius. Over eons genius has spoken through nature as well as supernatural beings such as gods, goddesses, spirits, animals, and mythical creatures. As children we reveled in that part of our nature; we played house and horse, indulging the voice of genius that expressed itself in a myraid of ways. Most often those ways were fantasies and daydreams, flights into a nonordinary reality in which we played for hours oblivious to the surrounding environment, the voice of adults, our parents' commands. Usually, we were accused of "not paying attention" or of "not listening." But we were listening. It's just that we heard and heeded a reality from which adults had long ago estranged themselves. We still had the ability to straddle two worlds. We could enter the world of fantasy at will and be at home there while not totally rejecting the world of adult reality. As Bruno Bettelheim, the great child psychologist, puts it, "And while a grove in a park may be experienced at times as a deep, dark forest full of hidden secrets, the child knows what it really is, just as a little girl knows her doll is not really her baby, much as she calls it that and treats it as such." In other words, when mother or father called us to dinner or some chore, we responded, perhaps not as promptly as they would have liked, but we easily moved from one state of reality into another, abandoning temporarily the world in which genius spoke for the world of everyday life where parents ruled.

Child psychologists, creativity researchers, and students of psychic phenomena have aptly demonstrated that children, usually between the ages of three and eleven, have an uncanny ability to tap into their genius, better than older children, and infinitely better than adults. Any parent knows this. Children are more imaginative, intuitive, playful, accepting, flexible, believing, and believable. Researchers have shown that children are also more receptive to hypnosis and extrasensory phenomena. Betty Edwards, in her manual *Drawing on the Right Side of the Brain,* suggests that a child's innate ability to draw both imaginatively *and* accurately is stifled around age eleven when the child feels adult pressure to represent the external world realistically. A child at this age will obsessively draw and redraw the same picture many times, trying for accuracy alone. Failing, most children give up seriously trying to learn to draw. The result is that most adults' drawing skills have not developed past that stage, even though their handwriting, mathematical abilities, reading knowledge, and other skills continue to improve with education.

Researchers have documented that the thinking of very young children is dominated by images and sensory impressions, feelings, and fantasies—the metaphors and feelings and images we tried to recapture in the last chapter. But in school, teachers consciously (but without consciously realizing the results) attempt to discourage imagery. Imagining and daydreaming are considered distractions from the more serious and "adultlike" learning that should be taking place. As psychologist Robert Sommer describes it, imagery becomes a "second-rate mode of thinking" and then "the deliberate elimination of visual thinking begins in earnest." According to his indictment, and it is one shared by many child psychologists, "sensory imagination declines during this period—not only from disuse but from deliberate discouragement by adults—save for those few young people seen as artistically talented." It reminds me of the belief, never proven and possibly unprovable, that small children really do see elves, but that when enough adult voices tell them there are no such things as elves, children eventually stop seeing them in order to be considered grown-up. Whether we actually saw them out there or only in our minds matters little. The truth is that we stopped believing in them and much that they represent: nonordinary reality, spirits, infinite possibilities, the playground of the creative imagination.

We have been speaking of genius as if it were a "person" or "voice" or another sentient, thinking self that is at once you and yet not totally you, since your personal genius taps the vast reservoir of collective wisdom that everyone can share. Do children unselfconsciously recognize and hear their personal genius? From every indication, it seems they do. It is interesting that many young children have an imaginary friend who plays with them, attends to them, gives them advice, counsels and consoles them when needed. As learning studies on children reveal, the imaginary friend seldom accompanies the child to school. If it does, it usually doesn't survive the first few months. As Sommer, Edwards, and others point out, the fantasy friend is systematically eliminated. Some children, however, may continue to talk and listen to their "friend" in the guise of a guardian angel or patron saint if encouraged to do so by religious training.

When many adults are asked about their imaginary childhood companions, they distinctly remember hearing their imaginary friends talk to them in the same quality of voice as that used by real people in their lives. But as they assumed the consciousness of adulthood and were trained to think and perceive like adults, they lost the ability to see, hear, and believe in that personal voice of genius. Some researchers, however, believe that human beings have an innate predisposition to have imaginary companions that can speak to them, comfort them, and advise them. Somewhere in the neurological structures of the dual hemispheres of the brain is rooted the genius that can take the voice of invisible playmates when we are children, and later when we are adults, it can speak as personal wisdom or intuition.

Creativity studies have shown the benefits of retaining childlike qualities into adulthood. The creative personality displays several key qualities that would ordinarily be labeled "childish" or "childlike"—gullibility, openness, a sense of wonder, enthusiasm, innocence, naiveté. Consider gullibility, a concept much maligned by the voice of adulthood. Silvano Arieti defines gullibility as the creative skill of "ruling out criticism and suspending judgment for a certain period of time." It includes an ability to recognize synchronicities. Gullibility "goes beyond accepting similarities as accidental or due to mere coincidence," Arieti explains. It means accepting similarities or synchronicities as having meaning, as embodying "certain underlying orderly arrangements in everything beyond and within us." The creative person trains himself or herself to discover the underlying orderly arrangements. We must become gullible once again. We must be willing to explore everything, to stand innocently before the universe, not rejecting anything. We need to stand in front of Thoreau's cave and seriously consider the possibility that elves might live there. We must occasionally regard the dark grove of trees in the forest as the possible haunt of gods and goddesses. We must, in short, peer into our unconscious, looking for genius and ready to hear it.

The purpose of this chapter is twofold.

First, to hear the voice of genius we need to temporarily silence the voice of adulthood. To do this we must "recognize" our personal childhoods. "Recognize" literally means to "know again." Some of the exercises in this chapter will take you back into your childhood and unlock memories and moments that have long been buried in your unconscious. Our personal childhoods still harbor insights, dreams, hopes, visions, and expectations that can electrify our humdrum adult lives. Our childhoods are like encyclopedias about ourselves that we closed too early and never finished reading. Now is the time to open them again. Now that we are adults, we can gain a clearer perspective not only of childhood but also of adulthood by recalling our childhood dreams and wishes.

Second, some of the exercises are structured to recapture childlike perceptions of reality. We all yearn for our future and our yearning has roots in childhood, still expressed in attitudes and perceptions that we discarded years ago, thinking them childish and foolish. Yet we can still use them creatively by playing gullible or naive or innocent or adventurous for a time. We can once again hear the voice of genius that speaks so vividly through dreams, visions, and images. We still have a future to plan, dreams to dream, further stages of maturity to enter. So as adults, let's "adopt the child," that is, the attitude of a child. The old adage that youth is wasted on the young has much truth in it.

Recognizing Your Personal Childhood

To know again your personal childhood requires effort and honesty—effort to unlock memories that have lain dormant over the years, honesty to accept those memories be they pleasant or fearsome. Many dormant memories are inactive precisely because they are traumatic ones which we have repressed. Some of us relive them in nightmares. Some of us never encounter them again. No one wants to live in a past filled with fear, pain, suffering, guilt, or resentment. Nevertheless, if those experiences were there, they continue to operate in our psyches below the conscious level. They are still part of us, and they are also part of our genius. They have something to say about ourselves, our world, the way we perceive life around us, the way we treat others. They may even influence our decisions, choices, and plans for the future. We must accept them honestly and deal with them.

But for most people, childhood was not one long bitter experience. In spite of the traumatic moments, our youthful days held joyous, happy, exuberant experiences as well. Chances are there were as many—if not more—healthy and memorable experiences as unhealthy ones. Many of these, too, slip into a corner of our unconscious where they lie forgotten. It's unfortunate we do not recall them more often, because our adult reveries about childhood joys may be the precise antidote we need to counteract the deleterious effects of our less happy memories.

EXERCISE:

Youthening

In T. H. White's *The Once and Future King*, old Merlin the magician tells Arthur that, contrary to most human experience, he "youthens" rather than ages. He began as an old soul who grows continually younger over the centuries, until, as Thoreau would say, he will be "as wise as the day he was born." A high degree of wisdom in Thoreau's estimation! Here is an exercise that will have remarkable results as you practice it.

First, relax, breathe deeply, get comfortable, light a candle or a stick of incense, darken the room, put on hypnotic flute music or use whatever technique you like to put yourself in a meditative mode. Then begin with your present age and count slowly backward. Obviously some of us will take longer at this exercise than others! Keep counting, averaging about one year every two or three seconds, or one year every slow, deep breath. Empty your mind as you do this, trying to think of nothing but the numbers themselves. Go all the way back to age one.

Then begin again. This time let images arise spontaneously as you count backward. Don't hold onto any particular one, but keep counting, letting other images come and go as they please. Eventually, you will stir up images of incidents, situations, people you knew and things you did at various ages of your life. Many of these will be favorite memories that have stayed with you over the years. But as you do this exercise, you will notice younger memories emerge: people, places, incidents you haven't thought about in a long time. You'll be surprised how many images and memories from your teens and childhood will present themselves. Don't worry if on later reflection you realize that a particular memory didn't coincide exactly with the age you were counting at the moment. That's not important.

Perform this exercise several times a day, whenever you have a quiet or relaxed moment. After a week or so, you'll have brought back many memories. As you do this exercise, merely note the images that appear. Don't dwell on them at this time, or you may break their power to stir up related memories. Later you can use them for more extended reflection or for writing about in your journal.

What can the voice of genius say to you in this exercise? Plenty. Your genius speaks from that treasure trove of dreams, visions, memories, experiences that are not always conscious. You may discover in your "youthening" that attitudes and values you thought you discarded still operate within you. They can still fire up old enthusiasms. You may want to reincorporate some of these values more consciously into your adult worldview as you recognize them as important aspects of your personality.

This exercise may work better for older people, not just because they have more years to count back! Rather, from a Jungian perspective, the first half of your life is dedicated to individuating yourself and learning how to function in society as a unique, separate individual. It is an extremely present- and future-oriented time in your life. The latter half of one's life, say from age thirty-five or so onward, has different concerns more compatible with this exercise. It is a time of reflection on the past and preparation for death. It is a time of reverie, of assessment, or reviewing the past and making the best use of the time ahead. So in these years our general thrust is not to break from and forget childhood and adolescence but to remember it and learn from it. Counting backward may teach us lessons we were too busy to learn as we went through those years of defiance, breaking away, rejecting childish things.

Tell Me a Story

Genius has many stories to tell you, but your adult voice may discourage you from listening because most of them you have already heard. Fortunately, they are good ones and worth repeating. They are the rich old folk legends, myths, and fairy tales which, like good literature the world over, are worthy of retelling and rehearing until we die. For each time we re-encounter the great tales of the ages, genius discovers new truths, or perhaps it's more accurate to say old truths that become new for us once again.

Much of a child's waking and dreaming life is dominated by fairy tales, legends, and fantasies. Children need the "larger than life" images of heroes, villains, gods and goddesses, elves, gnomes, and supernatural creatures of all shapes, stripes, and shiftings. While it's true that fairy tales do not describe external reality as adults perceive it, they do describe the internal reality of the psyche, even the adult psyche, as seen so frequently in dreams peopled with dragons, damsels in distress, knights in armor, or creatures and demons of unspeakable horror. Of course, our nightly dreams can also present joys and exhilarating adventures of flying and heroic deeds that leave us waking in the morning regretting we could not sleep a few hours longer.

The world of fairy tales is the world of the interior, the world of the heart, of genius. Both G. K. Chesterton and C. S. Lewis suspected that fairy tales were "spiritual explorations" that revealed "human life as seen, or felt, or divined from the inside." As we saw in our discussion of the voice of reason, the interior world of imagination and creativity is a world of image and metaphor. Images never stay put. They slide around, shift their shapes and meanings, turn into other things with all the magic and mystery of the beings and creatures we find in fairy tales. By placing our minds within the world of fairy tales, we force ourselves to visualize another reality, to "divine life from the inside," where the voice of genius speaks. Have you ever noticed how the formulaic beginning for most fairy tales and sacred myths immediately puts the listener into a nonordinary reality? Once upon a time . . . in a country far away . . . a long time ago in a galaxy far, far away. . . . The time is a sacred one, not bound to ordinary reality or the external world as we know it.

To contemplate the world of fairy tales means to contemplate the world of archetypal patterns and images where genius lives and moves. According to Carl Jung, we all share certain archetypes of primal images, no matter what culture we grow up in. Our dreams and fantasies produce them: the young hero, the wise old man or woman, the seductress, the virgin, the dark cave, the night journey, the sacred talisman, the anima/animus figures, the shadow demons. Different cultures express these primitive images in various ways. As human beings we experience the meaning and power of archetypes and give them some conscious shape. For indeed, archetypes are symbols and images with power—power to transform ourselves, our perceptions, our beliefs, our understanding of the universe. Learning to listen to genius means learning how to accept these archetypes consciously, how to work with them, how to use them in your daily life for wisdom and insight.

EXERCISE:

Once Upon a Time

If you have an old collection of fairy tales, myths, folk legends, try re-reading them. They probably will not hold your attention at first as would a juicy romance or spy thriller, so don't try to read them all at once or for a long sitting. Read them slowly, piecemeal, meditatively, a few pages or episodes at a time. Think about them during the day. Make them the focus of formal relaxation or contemplation. (You don't have to chant OM all the time!) Or recite them for yourself if you remember them. Use visualization techniques to see, hear, and experience the adventures you can recall from memory. As in other visualization exercises, make your images as sensuously rich as possible.

Or, in your journal, rewrite your own version of the fairy tales that meant the most to you as a kid.

With a friend or with several friends at a party, ask each person to relate the fairy tale or legend that was his or her favorite when a child. Then ask yourself or another person what about the tale was so exciting or appealing. Which character did you identify with the most?

Some therapists actually use this technique to get a person to rethink personal childhood values, dreams, wishes, and disappointments. The fact that we can still remember our favorite tales indicates that their themes still contain important information about who we are: we want to discover buried treasure, we want to be rescued by a handsome prince, we want to slay dragons, we want to fly, we want to be part of a band of outlaws, we want to run off to sea, we want to live in the woods or an enchanted palace. Fairy tales are not just the stuff of kids' dreams. They are ours. We have twisted them, perhaps, distorted and shrunk their larger-than-life images, discounted their powerful meanings as we stopped telling them. But as soon as you say, "My favorite bedtime story was about. . .," you have just unlocked a world of meaning and energy that can still serve you creatively. It can still be the world of energy and imagery in which you hear the voice of genius.

Rites of Passage

The major turning points of our lives—adolescence, marriage, mid-life crisis—are often difficult times. But the fact is, you have already made it through many of the rites of passage in your life. You have survived, even prevailed! As you look back on your past triumphs and defeats, you should be able to glean for yourself what your own personal secret is. Is it luck? Perseverance? Help from your friends? Faith? Blood, sweat, and tears? All of the above? You have managed to cope in some fashion or other. We can gain insight into how our genius has been guiding us over the years by studying the major turning points in our earlier lives. But let's not just rehash them as we would ordinarily do. Let's turn our previous lives into epics.

EXERCISE:

The Epic of My Life

Robert Frost was accused of turning the most ordinary event in his life into heroic terms. Perhaps he did, but it made wonderful poetry. Consider the topics of his poems: walking through woods, looking at snow, cleaning the pasture spring, bringing in a horse, chopping wood. When you read Frost's poetry, everything seems to take on heroic proportions, endowed with incredible significance and meaning. Let's do Frost one better.

In your journal make a list of the major events in your life in ordinary terms: graduating, falling in love, getting married, your first job, moving out from your parents' home, leaving town, running away, getting fired, switching careers, the birth of your children, divorce, death of loved ones, becoming ill, your children leaving home, and so forth. Then select one that appeals to you at the moment. You can work on the others later. Does it remind you of any classic folk tale or fairy tale or scriptural passage or fictional character or even a favorite movie? The closer you can mirror your life event with a truly epic story the better. If you can turn yourself, the people involved, the places, the events into heroic terms, writing it on a grand scale, you will activate the archetypal images that were truly involved when it occurred.

Whether you realize it or not these are the unconscious images that continue to churn in your psyche even when you're not consciously thinking about that event. Once we have lived events, they take their places along with the heroes, villains, demons, enchanted and threatening places that have resided in our unconscious since the days of childhood. A common experience of how the epic world of the unconscious and the humdrum world of ordinary reality meet is at night when you wake and realize that the ogre, wicked queen, or dashing pirate you were dreaming about were your boss, your mother-in-law, or the young man who works in data processing. Images slip around and none is completely isolated from the others.

By visualizing the high and low points of our past lives, either in meditation exercises or by transcribing them in journals, we begin to see how genius has helped us in the past. We also see how on occasion we have refused that help or ignored the voice of genius. The point of this exercise is not to fill you with regret or remorse. There is no sense in resuffering past defeats, but you can reconsider them as the components of your own personal mythology, the cast of characters and incidents that when "writ large" do transform your memory of them into images and metaphors you can now understand. In doing so, you hear the voice of genius explaining the lessons or meanings you may not have derived from them the first time around.

The Imp of the Perverse

In his tale "The Imp of the Perverse," Edgar Allan Poe relates the overwhelming desire on the part of a criminal to reveal the fact that he has pulled off the perfect crime. This intriguing theme has been retold many times: If someone can successfully commit the perfect crime, would he feel the need for recognition so strongly that the Imp of the Perverse would convince him to shout, "*I* did it!"? We have all grown up with an Imp of the Perverse dwelling in our consciences. A little voice that says, "Go ahead! Do it—even though it may ruin your life!"

It is as if there is still a bad little child locked within us who wants to defy our parents' commands not to do this or that. There is nothing wrong in pleasing one's parents—within limits. As we mature, we realize that if we are to live our own lives independently of our parents we may have to go against some of their wishes and defy injunctions laid down as law when we were children. Times change, and the mores of yesteryear don't always keep pace with modern reality.

One of the insidious by-products, however, of having been raised by strong-minded parents is that often pleasing them meant being passive. To gain their approval we often had to stop doing or give up what we really wanted. We were told it was for our own good, that we would succeed better in society, or that "good little boys or girls" didn't do that. True, every child needs to be socialized; that is, something in our original nature needs to be tamed and trained to survive in the society and culture into which we were born. Everyone needs to create a social ego that understands what is allowed and what is denied. But if our social ego becomes a restrictive mask through which the adult voice tells us what to do and what not to do, what to think, believe in, or value, it can ultimately stifle our creativity. Genius speaks from our deepest desires and wishes whether they be socially acceptable or not. As we listen to our genius, we should learn which of these desires are truly unsociable or "uncivilized" and which are only labeled such because we are still trying to be our parents' good little child.

EXERCISE:

Making Friends with the Imp

As you recognize your personal childhood in these exercises, make a list of the things that parents or authority figures told you never to do—particularly the ones that predicted you would be a failure in life. Obviously, we are not considering serious moral offenses such as murder, rape, theft, arson, cheating, and the time-honored commandments which if not obeyed would truly make society unlivable. Instead, we are looking for attitudes that could be tolerated under the right circumstances and might even need to be engaged in at times for purposes of creativity. For example, "Saving for a rainy day." "Never question authority." "Boys don't cry." "Girls must want to get married and raise children." "Never change careers." "Accept your lot without complaining." Sometimes even the most trivial parental commands stay with us into adulthood: "Never eat in bed." "Don't skip breakfast." "Don't go outside in winter without a hat." "Wash the car once a week." "Don't paint the living room orange."

The point of this exercise is to re-evaluate your fears, particularly the ones that stifle creativity and change, the ones that keep you locked into set ways of living and thinking. Creativity studies show that "deviant thinking" is a characteristic shared by most creative personalities. No one is encouraging you to throw all moral and socially acceptable behavior to the winds. Rather, determine which attitudes and values are really crucial to your social life. Which are essential? Which are not? Which have been blocking you from self-expression? Which prevent you from living a more creative and satisfying life?

What Do You Want to Be When You Grow Up?

Most of us have already answered that question many times. Some of us have actually become what we wanted to be when we grew up. Some of us are still striving for it, even at age forty or sixty. It is not simply a question of career; it is deeper than that. It goes back to what impressed you as a child, what you were "programmed" to become, how you acquiesced in the plan that unfolded for you, whether you resisted it, how you determined your own path and forged the adult personality you have now become out of the little girl or boy you used to be. We are all a composite of what others, circumstances, fate, and we ourselves made out of our lives—and what we continue to make. In her book on intuition, Frances E. Vaughan says, "Learning to listen to the inner voice of awakened intuition is appropriate at every age. Everyone has a chronological age, and everyone is also timeless. The essential being who you were as a baby and who you are today remains always the same." How can we discover the essential being, that original nature, that primitive ancestor who is "parent" to our "child"? Vaughan suggests an exercise in self-understanding that may help you discover the essential you. As in the preceding exercise, in this one you must indulge your Imp of the Perverse and peel off layers of your self, like an onion, giving up aspects of your personality that you may consider essential for success.

EXERCISE:

Stripping Down to the Essential You

Vaughan's suggestion is to write on nine or ten strips of paper all the essential attributes, roles, phrases, and terms that define you. They may involve your relationships (mother, brother, parent); your career, position, or professional reputation; personality traits (friendly, shy, aggressive); or values and habits (affluence, determination, education, good health, exercise, reading, travel). Think about these seriously for some time so that you weed them down to the nine or ten essentials. Then stack them in order of importance with the most important on the bottom. Next, either alone in a meditative mood, or with a partner whom you can trust and share this with, consider what would happen if you had to eliminate the top strip of paper from your life, your personality, your very being. What would you then be like? How would you be different? What in your life would change? Who would you be without it? Give your reactions serious thought. Try to explain them as fully as possible either to yourself or a friend. Experience what you would be like without this quality or role. Proceed through the list until you have stripped away the last attribute. Who are you then? Is this your original nature?

Then reverse the procedure, putting on each role, position, quality, or definition of yourself until you are back together again. There is no right or wrong way to do this. The entire exercise is one of self-awareness, a method to clear away the masks you wear and face honestly the most essential question of your life no matter what your age: Who are you?

Who Do You Want to Be Like?

In *The Uses of Enchantment,* Bruno Bettleheim suggests that the child identifies with the hero or heroine of a story not because the character is morally good (although heroes usually are good) but rather because the child projects him or herself wholeheartedly into that one character. Everything that character is and does appeals to the child. It serves as a role model for children at the age when they imitate either adults or older children, trying on personalities like new clothes, seeing which fit, which don't, trying to decide who they want to be like.

Over the years we have decided what we want to be like and that is how we are. But is it possible to be different? To behave differently? To think differently? Is it still possible even as adults to try on other masks, other types of behavior, adapt personality traits different from our own? Here is an exercise that will be both a discovery in self-awareness and a process by which you can act differently on occasion from your usual style and to your advantage.

EXERCISE:

Inventing Your Behavior

You may want to do this exercise with a tape recorder so that you can play it back and listen to your new behavior. If not, simply do it out loud sometime when you are alone, or listen to yourself with your inner ear.

Imagine that you have been seated in a restaurant by an impertinent maître d', and now after twenty minutes no one has waited on you, brought you a menu, or given you glasses of water or bread to munch on. You're becoming furious. Others who arrived after you already have their soup! The headwaiter is about to pass your table. You motion him to come over.

Now into your tape recorder say what you will tell him, but assume that you are timid and shy and oh so polite! Now change characters. Assume you are a well-known public official who is accustomed to prompt and flawless service. Then become a foreign tourist unfamiliar with American customs and language. Next assume you are an easygoing, laid-back type. Then assume you will make the headwaiter laugh while at the same time making your point that you want service.

If you want more clear-cut models to determine how you will behave in this situation, imagine that you are the President or First Lady, Dickens' Scrooge, Mother Theresa of Calcutta, Richard III, Scarlett O'Hara or Melanie. Make your performance as complete as possible. Experience the feelings and emotions, imagine the train of thought each of your characters would use, what arguments would appeal to each, what threats, and so forth.

The purpose here is not to go around impersonating famous or fictional characters, but to meet the "you" that perhaps you could have become under different life circumstances. The exercise is also good rehearsal for situations where you want to emote or argue more effectively and in a style that is not typically your own. It's somewhat similar to the parent feigning more anger than he or she really feels to make an impression upon a child. There is an element of make-believe about it, true, but then there are situations in which you could operate more successfully if you could manipulate the impression you make on others more effectively. In some ways, we still have more social roles to learn. We are still asking the question, "What or who do I want to be like?"

Life will not hold still. New changes, new passages in our lives await us. Who do you want to be like when your children leave home? Who do you want to be like when you retire? Who will you be like when your spouse dies? Throughout life we are called upon to play many roles. Genius helps us develop the roles. The more we recognize our essential nature and distinguish it from the social masks we wear, the better we will be at wearing the masks when necessary and removing them to be authentically ourselves.

Being an imposter for a day, rehearsing behavior that is not typical of you, playing "dress-up"—in a sense it is all a reversion to childhood experiences when you were confronted with new situations calling upon your inner resources to invent the behavior, the mask, the persona that was required. Over the years many of these masks and personas became fixed. The question before us as we listen to our genius is: Should they remain fixed? Or is our genius trying to tell us that some changes should be made?

Healing Images and Image Healing

Genius has the ability to heal. Through the use of healing imagery, we can heal our psyches and our physical bodies. In clinics across the nation, health-care personnel are learning that imagery can relieve distress, cause disease to go into remission, cure illness, and heal the patient. It has been documented that visualizing the body producing additional enzymes or the immune system fighting off a virus can actually speed up recovery. EEG and respiratory data, blood pressure readings, muscle tensions, skin temperature, and other monitoring techniques show that a healing image held in the conscious mind can produce beneficial effects upon the body. The amazing thing for us as we study the use of childhood to hear the voice of genius is that it doesn't matter how fanciful or childlike the imagery is. One patient might visualize an army of soldiers trooping through her bloodstream firing laserbeam ray guns at a viral infection, which she may picture as ugly ants. Another patient might visualize a ball of blue light, whose luminescence has magical healing properties, floating through the parts of his body that need curing. Still another patient might visualize a mystical element in the air that he breathes and with every breath "see" this ethereal medicine enter his lungs and course throughout his bloodstream. No matter how unsophisticated the image is, it has the power to heal if the patient believes in the process and uses it properly.

Instructors in visualization techniques such as these point out that if the image is powerful enough, that is, if it has meaning and significance for the individual, it continues to hover in the background of his or her consciousness, even when the person is not attending to it directly. But often the person does consciously attend to it off and on during the day. Much like an affirmation or a consoling line from scripture or an inspiring line of verse, a healing image has the power to calm the nerves, adjust the autonomic nervous system, produce a relaxed state, and in general regulate the body and mind during periods of stress.

It is not so fanciful, therefore, for adults to retain the childhood images that meant so much to them when they were younger. It is true that we will not have the adventures of a Robin Hood, never truly meet a Prince Charming, slay the evil witch or dragon, or engage in spectacular feats of strength and prowess as the heroines and heroes of our fairy tales once did. Nevertheless, if we continue to identify with them, even on a subconscious level, they have the power to revive our spirits, remind us of our original nature, give us a sense of playfulness, and renew our hopes that, as in our youth, there is more life to live, more things "to be when we grow up."

If you are in the habit of meditating or focusing on an image as a form of relaxation, try old fairy tale heroes. Or recite the lyrics of a childhood song or verse that you enjoyed when young. The mantra which you chant to yourself or concentrate on in meditation does not have to be an esoteric word or phrase discovered in a book on Eastern mysticism. It might very well be a nonsense jingle from your childhood that has the power to bring back the feelings and memories through which your genius can speak.

EXERCISE:

Chanting Enchantment

The words "enchantment" and "chant" come from the Latin root word that means "to sing." The word "incantation" is also related. All these terms taken together suggest something we hardly think about, yet can recognize the truth of almost every day: the power of song, melody, and rhyme to put us into another state of consciousness. We become mesmerized by a term repeated over and over. We slip into a light trance by chanting a phrase over and over. We summon up gods or spirits of genius by the constant repetition of a word or lyric. Have you noticed children singing the same phrase again and again until it drives you nuts? Have you noticed how children can almost hypnotize themselves by repeating the same action? Where are their minds at these times? What creatures or spirits do they see and hear? We often associate such behavior only with very young children, but we all have the ability to slip into an altered state of consciousness at will if we take the time to create the appropriate conditions. Perhaps you have already experienced self-mesmerization when you doodle on a pad of paper, jog around a track, or watch telephone poles go by while riding in a car.

It may help if you sit in a semi-darkened room, focus your attention on a candle flame, a crystal, or a spot on the wall. You can heighten the enchantment, the non-ordinariness, of the setting by burning incense. Soft music may work, too. Use whatever method you like to relax. Then choose a phrase, image, word, or song, and begin chanting it either out loud or silently in your inner ear. Continue this for fifteen to twenty minutes or more.

Were your brain waves and other autonomic responses monitored, you would see that you have put yourself into a state of relaxation similar to that immediately before you fall asleep. You might even fall asleep! But that is not the goal. It is at these times of mindless reverie when genius speaks. It is precisely in this process of clearing your mind for the enchanting effect of the repeated phrase or melody that fresh ideas are born, new insights burst from their state of incubation, and deeper perceptions of who you are begin to form. You'll find that when you end the exercise and return to ordinary reality, you'll have more energy, a clearer mind, and more mental stamina. Many people claim that fifteen minutes of chanting or self-mesmerizing like this is more refreshing and beneficial than thirty minutes of napping.

Whether you use relaxation and visualization strategies such as this for physical or psychic healing, you'll find a general sense of improved well-being. The mind and body are interrelated so intimately that it is difficult, if not impossible, to separate the purely physical from the purely mental. As we noted earlier, genius speaks on the mental, physical, emotional, and spiritual levels, sometimes all at once. Exercises such as this will demonstrate to you that these four planes are not actually different dimensions but more like four interrelated, spiraling types of energy that twist around each other, penetrate each other, and reinforce the primary flow of energy that you call your life.

The Imaginary Friend Revisited

Many people are reluctant to admit that they had an imaginary companion when young. Some who will admit it, however, are nevertheless hesitant to suggest that they actually heard it speak to them! As if to hear voices is always a mark of insanity! Yet everyone has the ability to see and hear phenomena internally even though they hesitate to admit it publicly. Some indulge in their interior world of reality more frequently and more successfully than others. We usually think of these people as creative personalities.

But their secret is not so mysterious. It is to listen to one's genius and learn to live with that genius as a companion. Use the preceding exercises that took you back into your childhood and lured you into adopting the attitude of a child as a kind of imaginary playground where you can meet your genius. Think of your genius as a companion who exists on a nonordinary plane of reality. If you remember your imaginary friend from childhood, use that image for your genius. If your companion was an animal, spirit, or supernatural being or mythical character, your genius will not object to being thought of, talked to, sought after in those terms. Ultimately it doesn't matter to your genius. It is already part of you. It can be the childlike part of you as well as the adult part of you, and it may even communicate more forthrightly and naturally on the childlike level. Our childhood persona is closer to our original nature, less encumbered with the roles we have adopted in order to conform to society.

So rediscover your childhood companion. Name it genius. And listen to what genius has to say, no matter how much it sounds like something you used to know as a child.

4 | Trust in the Gray

". . . Things are infinitely more complicated, and right and wrong do not stand separately, any more than black and white do in nature. . . . Don't think of the future as a blackness nor as a dazzling light—it will be better to trust in the gray."

—VINCENT VAN GOGH

Black and white, right and wrong, up and down, male and female, night and day—even left brain and right brain! The mind works quickly and easily with polarities. It feels comfortable with opposing categories. How much easier it is when there are only two choices: column A and column B. It's a very limited choice, but the poverty of selection makes the choice easier. Less to think about, less to evaluate, less to be uncertain about. And less to learn.

It is a natural mental function to imagine an equal and opposite category for almost any person, place, thing, quality, virtue, or vice. Brain research has shown that this function takes place primarily on the left side of the brain, the same side that controls rational, linear thought. A polarized worldview appeals to the timid, who, unlike van Gogh, are not comfortable with gradations of gray, areas that are ambiguous and defiant of rigid categorization. Trapped in their established values and perceptions, these people are quick to make judgments, because for them there is little to be wary about. The world is clear. It's either this or that.

We see examples of this dichotomized thinking in many areas of life. Have you ever noticed how uncomfortable most Americans are whenever a strong third political party emerges? Actually there has never been a time in American history when there was not a third or fourth party, but our traditional myth is that there should be only two. One of the psychologically satisfying effects of watching a football or baseball game is that for a few hours, the complex universe is reduced to two distinct choices. You can immediately and unquestioningly declare your loyalty, your enthusiasm, your voice. In the world of geopolitics, it has become fashionable since World War II to view the entire world as divided into two camps—the Soviet Union's sphere vs. what we call the "Free World." Unaligned nations are, in this schema, a threat, not to be trusted, sly, unwilling to declare their loyalties. In fact, many Americans automatically assume that a Third World nation's refusal to take sides is an admission that its sympathies lie with the Soviet Union. In our own society we have frequently divided up a multicomplex nation into misleading polarities: white and black, young and old, male and female, believers and unbelievers, true Americans and UnAmericans, capitalism and socialism, urban and rural, and so on.

In reality, of course, the world is more complex. There are areas of gray. In his study *The Natural Mind,* Andrew Weil noted that people who live along what he calls the "topography of Straightland" tend to perceive differences between things rather than similarities. In "Stonesville," however, citizens accept the ambivalent nature of reality and thus perceive similarities. As Weil defines it, ambivalence is "the co-existence of opposites that appear to be mutually antagonistic." The key word here is "appear." Indeed, there appear to be opposites but they need not always be mutually exclusive. Weil's faith in the healing power of ambiguity lets him assert that "any quality can be neutralized by combining it with its opposite in equal strength; the principle applies to love and hate as well as to positron and electron." This challenge to forget about contradictions and leap forward into the gray area, even morally, has always been exciting to some and threatening to others. The "realist" will doubt that the world is made that way; the visionary will affirm that the world is or can become that way.

Believing and living in the midst of ambiguities is challenging and liberating. It releases us from the trap of categorical thinking, a trap we can't leave until we know we are in it. Genius, speaking from the source of creativity, transcends polarities, unites opposites, and reconciles what appears to be contradictory. Genius uses categories but is not confined to them. When necessary, genius can leap beyond them.

You yourself have had personal examples of this leap that perhaps you weren't aware of. Think back to a poem which seemed confusing, unclear, ambiguous the first time you read it. Then on the second or third reading, or maybe while you were mulling it over while doing something else, a line or phrase suddenly flashed across your consciousness and you knew exactly what the poet was trying to tell you. Or more likely, you may have discovered one of the things the poem was trying to tell you, since often a poet doesn't realize all the meaning and insights he or she packs into a poem. Creative ambiguity is what makes a poem rich with meaning and worthy of many re-readings. John Keats called the state of mind that can live with ambiguity "negative capability"; that is, poet and reader must slip into a state of awareness in which they are "capable of being in uncertainties, mysteries, doubts; without any irritable reaching after facts and reason." When you become capable of "negative capability," you feel at home with doubt and uncertainty. You make friends with ambiguity and mystery. You are ready for the sudden insights and perceptions genius will flash across your mind.

"Capable of being in uncertainties, mysteries, doubts."

Keats' prescription for intuitive, poetic understanding is indeed threatening because we feel much safer with certainty, facts, and reason. The voice of doubt prevents us from believing in certain things, from perceiving relationships, from understanding the fluid and malleable nature of reality. It prevents us from taking the necessary steps to transform our lives. It keeps us awake at night! Doubt is insidious, eating away at our peace of mind, gnawing like a termite to bring the well-wrought mansion of certitude crashing down around us. But, if we make doubt an ally we can spring free of the trap in which our current mode of thinking is caught.

In this chapter we will learn some strategies to silence the voice of doubt and make it our ally.

Trust in the Gray

It is better to trust in the gray, says van Gogh. For some of us it's hard to even find the gray. Our thinking is so locked into opposing categories that to imagine options lying between them takes a mental or imaginative leap of which we aren't capable. Have you ever wondered why some people "get to the point" faster than others? Why do some individuals need less information to reach conclusions while others need mountains of data? Why do some folks *never* get the point? In other words, if there is a quality or talent called "insightfulness," how is it distributed among human beings? Why do some have it and others don't? Studies have shown that intuition or insightfulness does not relate to academic ability or the traditional skills taught in school. Rather, people who rank high on insightfulness tend to be unconventional in their thinking and their lives. They are not locked into the conventional categories, values, and attitudes of the average person.

Here's an example that should help you recognize this illusive quality called insight. Remember the riddle that goes: "A big Indian and a little Indian were sitting on a fence. The little Indian is the son of the big Indian, but the big Indian is not the father of the little Indian." Now while you're thinking about that, consider this one: "There is a man at home and he is wearing a mask. Another man is coming home but he is not wearing a mask. They are not related to each other, but they know each other. What is going on?"

Like most riddles, these involve categorical thinking. The riddle-maker banks on the average person thinking in rather fixed stereotypes. A person who takes a long time to solve a riddle like this is probably one whose thinking is hedged in by stereotyped categories and prejudgments. Speedy riddle solvers exercise a willing suspension of disbelief. They temporarily ignore their categories, stereotypes, judgments, and beliefs in what is possible and impossible. Then the gray areas where riddle answers lurk grow clear. The solution sharpens, and they discover that it sits in some unconventional category or an unlikely spot between categories.

The answer to the Indian riddle is that the big Indian is the *mother* of the little Indian. The riddle works because when the average American hears the word "Indian," images of warriors, braves, and chiefs spring to mind. Another misleading clue in the riddle is the phrase "sitting on a fence." The common assumption is that men and boys sit on fences, but women or girls don't.

The second riddle is about baseball. Need I say more? If you were stumped, it was due to an erroneous prejudgment. You assumed "home" meant the house where the man lived, not "home plate." In solving riddles, the first tactic is to suspend all meanings, categories, and judgments about the key words in the riddle. You might still be stumped. But chances are, you'll get the point faster when you do solve it.

EXERCISE:

Getting Unstumped

This exercise is simple and fun. Buy a book of riddles and practice. As with crossword puzzles and murder mysteries, the more you read and work them, the better you'll get. What will happen is that you'll learn to suspend judgment and forget old categories.

Here is another exercise for learning to deal with ambiguity. If you make this exercise part of your weekly routine, you'll fill your imagination with alternative realities, categories, and phenomena that will make it harder for you to stay stuck in the old trains of thought.

EXERCISE:

Strange Worlds

Get into the habit of reading science fiction, tales of the supernatural, or fairy tales, as suggested in the last chapter. It is good to soak your imagination in "unbelievable" plots, characters, places, situations. This doesn't mean you have to give up good literature for trash. There are highly respected writers in all these fields, but trash works, too! Literature of any kind is in some sense "escapist," but that's not always negative. If you use it to escape into new ways of relating to your daily world and new ways of perceiving reality, you will be able to handle the ambiguities of your own life more successfully.

Letting the Category Out of the Bag

Each of us walks around with a mind stuffed with categories. Some we are aware of, others need pointing out. For example, every St. Patrick's Day, someone on the Irish side of my family proudly points out, to the chagrin of those on the German side, that the world is divided into two types of people: those who are Irish and those who wish they were. At some point in my childhood I probably believed in these two categories, but I soon learned that very few people in the world live by them even on St. Patrick's Day! For those who do, these are very personal categories. We'll see in a moment how each of us has similar though different ones.

We place items in categories based on similarities and dissimilarities. Our brains are marvelous tools in this regard. They let us classify phenomena and group certain objects together, which saves us from having to rethink every situation. But the brain is also a deceptive tool, in that it can easily lead to mistakes, seeing differences where none exist or imagining similarities that are not really there. It appears, however, that the brain more often errs on the side of missing similarities rather than discovering too many. Perhaps that's why the really creative individuals are few in number. They perceive similarities that most of us overlook.

Here is an exercise to become more aware of how your mind discriminates and classifies.

EXERCISE:

Search and List

Make a list of ten things that are red. These should be items that are normally red or thought of as red, such as apples, rather than Buicks.

Next, list as many things as you can that are red, aromatic, and edible. Some of these may come from your first category of ten red things. You can also make two opposite categories of red things that stink and red things that are sweet-smelling. Strawberries and fire engines are now opposites, whereas in the first category they were similar.

Now list as many types of food as you can think of that begin with the letter P. This category is a subset of a larger category called food. It's also a purely linguistic category based on the English language. Your food items may have nothing else in common other than that they are indeed food and they begin with P.

List ten rivers you have either seen or crossed and ten rivers you have not seen or crossed. These categories are based on your personal experience and would not exist except for the fact that you are you.

List ten people you admire and ten people you despise. These two categories are based on moral judgments. You might find these two hard to fill. The more you think about someone the more you might realize you can't easily place him or her in either strictly defined category. You may find yourself wishing for some "gray ground" in between, or a continuum, or a scale of 1 to 10.

You see how the world can fall into categories, some arbitrary and artificial, others quite natural? Some items don't seem to belong totally in any one category or another, and when you try to squeeze them in, you discover that you have defined the category too narrowly or you are misreading similarities. If you find that you regularly perceive events and people in very fixed categories, chances are you are not listening to your genius. The creative personality is open to new associations and sees connections and similarities that others miss. You don't have to abandon all your categories, but you should become aware of the ones that color your perceptions about important matters. If you listen to your genius, you will discover how the world wants to break out of those groupings, how phenomena seek to relate to each other under new terms.

Professor E. H. Gombrich created an exercise to show how easily the mind can fall into classifying external reality on purely nonsense terms. Basing his strategy on the mind's penchant for seeing opposites and polarities, he suggests that you take two similar objects and put them into two categories you never knew existed.

EXERCISE:

Ping! Pong! . . . Poing!

The categories are ping and pong. (Poing is my personal category that I'll explain later.) Let's start with an easy one. An elephant and a gerbil. Which goes into ping and which into pong? Right, the elephant is definitely pong and the little gerbil is ping. How about a broadsword and a rapier? Pong and ping, respectively. What about Presidents Nixon and Carter? A tuba and a flute? How would you classify the members of your family? Don't engage in this exercise for too long. It can be dangerous. Most of all, don't tell any of your friends that you've done it.

If you are like most people, you'll quickly see how some categories can be nonsense. Polarities are tools of thought; they are instruments of perception, and sometimes they need fine tuning. We need to exercise a greater critical awareness. It is too easy to sort out the universe into polarities that don't mean anything, like ping and pong.

Genius is smarter, its perception more acute. Like Eastern sages explaining the yin and yang, genius sees that everything contains its opposite. In Eastern thought, all phenomena change constantly; all creation is in the process of becoming like its opposite which in fact it already contains. As Hegel taught, the process begins with a thesis, confronted by its antithesis, and results in a synthesis. The person who listens to genius becomes adept at joining together apparently contradictory qualities or reconciling opposites to produce a new reality. You may not restructure the government or discover the ultimate formula for the birth of the universe. The new reality might be simply a new vision for your own personal life, a new idea, a new goal, a fresh possibility. By redefining what you already know, by seeing things in unusual ways, by abandoning prior classifications, you may create the "poing!" You will realize that the world does not always fall into either column A or column B, but in reality there are C, D, E, and F columns and many more.

Neutralizing Opposites

Let's combine the hurricane thinking discussed in Chapter 2 with our tendency to perceive the world in terms of opposites. The exciting aspect of hurricane thinking is that it is unpredictable, and the depressing aspect of polarized thinking is that it is entrapping, limiting, and frequently misleading.

EXERCISE:

___

The Janus Blitz

Janus was the Roman god of doorways, thresholds, and arches. He had a face on each side of his head and could see the future and the past. He is also the god who rules the first month of the year, a time when one naturally looks back over the past year and anticipates the months ahead. His great power is simply his ability to see in two directions at once.

First, choose two opposites that have some important significance for you. They might be work related or social categories, or a political, religious, or moral divison by which you judge others. Then take a piece of paper and draw a line down the middle. Place one polarity in the center of each half and circle it, as we did for hurricane thinking. Then go at each one. You might work with each individually, or you might find it easier to let your mind blow from one side of the page to the other, jotting down related ideas as they come.

When you finish, see if any of the same attributes appear on both sides of the page. Circle these and connect them with a line. As you notice how many attributes are shared by each polarity, you may decide that the original dichotomy isn't as distinct as you had assumed. What's more, you will have a better understanding of the attributes that are significantly contradictory.

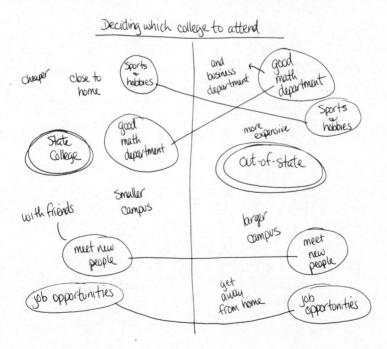

Next take two opposing aspects of the original polarities, perform the Janus Blitz on them and see what you come up with. Then do another set, and so on.

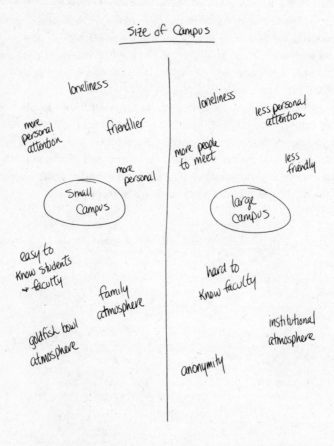

Like the ping and pong exercise, this one could go on indefinitely. Stop when you have distilled your categories of opposites so you can clearly see in what ways they are opposing and what ways they are not.

The Janus Blitz is a good exercise for practical problem solving and decision making when you're confronted with two alternatives that seem mutually opposed to each other, such as trying to decide where to spend a vacation, which of two jobs to take, or which college to go to. If they fall into opposition simply by virtue of their being your only choices, the Janus Blitz will help refine your decision and make a more critical judgment based on hidden options within each choice.

The Internal Split

Now that we've focused on the external world, let's look inside ourselves. Here too we discover polarities that split our own personalities. As with external reality, some of these internal dichotomies may appear to have more force and energy than they really possess. Others might turn out to be illusory. Many people confess that they often feel like two or more people, each at odds with the others. The dutiful son who would like to run away from home. The professional who would like to be less disciplined in her private life but knows that she has to be alert and ready for emergencies. The teacher who doesn't really believe in the value of his subject matter. The priest who envies the sinner. None of us are completely unified in our desires, wishes, public personas, and career choices. Walt Whitman warned his readers that he might "contradict" himself but not to worry because, as he said, "I contain multitudes."

And so do we all. While there is a connecting strand that holds our multiple personas together so that we can function predictably and reliably in private and public, there are also loose threads, looking for their own means of self-expression, seeking the hooks to which they might tie themselves and become anchored.

Your genius recognizes the multi-dimensional character of your life, realizes on levels that you may not be consciously aware of that there is more to you than the public self you wear out into the world each day and the private self that you can relax into when you're alone. The more you become conscious of these many faces with their unique and varied expressions, desires, and fears, the better you will understand yourself. Self-knowledge, like love in the old classic song, is a many splendored thing, because each individual self is many and splendored. The following exercise is an expedition into the many-layered composite that is you.

EXERCISE:

Face to Face

Select two opposing tensions in your life. These may be two contradictory urges or feelings, two incompatible goals, two roles you are required to play, perhaps two duties or responsibilities that are in conflict with each other. Some examples are: dependence and independence, career and family life, male and female, husband and father or mother and wife, freedom and security, friendship and solitude. Take a few minutes to discover the basic tension in your present life.

There are two methods to get these two sides of your self face to face.

First, in your journal write a dialogue or a movie or soap opera script between these two. Give them names. Create a conversation between the two in which each attempts to justify its position to the other. Or let the dialogue emerge from one's criticism of the other. For example, you may have the mother in you criticizing the wife for not spending enough time with her mate. You might let the businessman in you call the artist to task for not developing his skills. Create a running dialogue where the female aspect and male aspect of your psyche argue for supremacy or for a greater share in influencing your behavior.

A second way to get your selves face to face is to perform a Janus Blitz on the two aspects of your character. After you have exhausted all the associations and characteristics of each half, eliminate the ones that are shared by both. Then evaluate the remaining dissimilarities, the truly opposing forces in your psyche. Ask your genius for ways to reconcile these contradictions to bring them into closer harmony with each other. Think of them as possible allies, keeping in mind that in unity there is strength, and that since every quality contains its opposite, it is not a disadvantage to "contain multitudes." It is only self-defeating if the contradictions war with each other.

As in the economy, diversification is a strength. Whatever you discover within you in this exercise (do it regularly, each time using different aspects), consider it a strength. Genius can unite opposites. The warring factions within you can learn to reinforce each other, one supporting you in situations where the other is weak or ineffectual. For example, tolerance is a virtue, an asset in many circumstances, but there are times when one should be intolerant of injustice. The meek may inherit the earth, but the strong take heaven by storm. Life is too various for any one virtue or vice to dominate. There will be times when you need to tap into your genius for an equal and opposite power. Most likely that power is there, lying fallow, untapped, unsure of itself. Self-knowledge will help you unleash the energies you contain and harness them to conquer both heaven and earth.

Listening to Another's Genius

A friend was once accused of too much introspection. "It's unhealthy to be so concerned with yourself, always trying to understand what makes you tick!" he was told. Immediately he saw the truth of the statement, but it plunged him into even more self-absorption. He disappeared for three days trying to analyze why he was so preoccupied with himself! The same might be said of genius. Listen to it, but not exclusively. Listen also to the genius of others.

The following technique is a way to do that. It works best with another person (but it can prove beneficial for those who prefer to work alone). The other person can be a friend or a stranger. If you have the opportunity to do this exercise in a group, pair up with someone you don't know very well. It's not that a stranger's genius has more insight into your own nature, but often a stranger is more honest, fresh, and unbiased because he or she knows little or nothing about you. Once you collect impressions from a stranger, repeat the exercise with a friend and compare.

EXERCISE:

I See You

Sit across from your partner, relax, and look at each other for a few minutes, calmly and quietly. Take note of all the physical details you see in the face, the expression, the clothes, the hair, the position of the body, the state of tension or relaxation. Try to pick up psychological or spiritual clues, such as values, goals, secret thoughts, fears.

Then decide which one of you will go first. Begin by saying "I see you as a . . ." and complete the sentence with a specific example from as many of the nonhuman categories suggested below as the two of you have decided you will use.

The categories are: animals, plants, birds, colors, music, cars, novels, poetry, weather, landscapes, tools, movies, houses, streets, countries . . . and so on. Add other categories as you see fit.

So your partner might say, "I see you as a bluejay . . . a Mercedes Benz . . . a Roman villa . . . a Beethoven sonata . . . a Bergman movie . . . a Patti Page song . . . a Dickens novel . . . a country in Southeast Asia."

Ask how, why, in what ways. Have your partner explain as fully as possible. If he or she can't explain one, then just accept it as intuition but don't value it any less. "I just feel you are a Russian peasant" may be an intuitive statement that even without elaborate justification may explain more to you about yourself than a half dozen reasons why you are like a "pink flamingo." Accept each description of yourself as if it were true, particularly the ones that don't strike you immediately as accurate. Write them in your journal, or collect photos or illustrations of them and tape them to your bathroom mirror or leave them on your desk at work. At odd moments of the day reflect on them. Ask yourself how you are like them, or how you give these impressions to others. Observe yourself in situations where you adopt the behavior or characteristics of these images.

Ruminating on the information you learn from this exercise is a way of tapping into your genius. Remember, genius communicates in symbols and metaphors. The images given you by your partner may be new metaphors for behavior and personality traits you never considered before. If they are accurate, even to a small degree, they will become part of the dialogue between your social ego and your genius, a dialogue based on your images of yourself.

These images can also be used in helping you make decisions or take a course of action. For example, if you are wondering how to admonish your son or daughter over some matter, considering whether to take the authoritarian approach of a "Russian peasant" will provide unique insights regarding your success or failure that you might never have considered were you to just handle the matter in your usual style. As in the exercise "Inventing Your Behavior," you will discover other approaches which, whether you employ them or not, will allow you to evaluate the total situation more effectively.

Furthermore, by considering yourself in nonhuman terms you identify yourself with the nonhuman aspects of the universe. Consistently creative people perceive themselves as related intimately to the rest of reality. They have an almost primitive view of themselves as part of the whole creation. As the Sioux medicine man Black Elk explained about his people's worldview, there are "two-leggeds and four-leggeds." In other words, the creative person has a visionary mode of perception that sees herself or himself as one creature among many others.

The edge of our own personalities is not as sharply defined as we may believe. Intimacy and knowledge can extend to nonhuman beings (even inanimate objects) so that we perceive them less as "objects" for us to manipulate, control, or even destroy, and more as fellow "subjects" with whom we share the earth. As the Sioux say, "We are all relatives." It is a mystical viewpoint, but one from which genius speaks because it connects at some deep level with all other aspects of creation. To hear your genius you must share that point of view, believe in it, and, most importantly, experience it in daily life.

Dreams

One of the first questions people usually ask about dreams is what do they mean? You might ask this about the entire dream itself or the individual images and symbols the dream contains. Both are natural questions. Both lead the dreamer deeper into the dream and in the process deeper into his or her own psyche. The result is greater self-awareness.

Unlike the "I See You" exercise where you received images of yourself from another person, dreams produce your own images of yourself. Each night a psychic movie is played before your dream-eyes in which you see yourself, others in your life, fantastic creatures and situations, places you may remember from earlier years or places you have never been—all created for your nightly entertainment out of the "stuff" that is you. If in your dream you are a Russian peasant or a pink flamingo, it is not because someone else saw those qualities in you. It is because at some level of your identity those images have meaning for you. In a sense every dream has the same meaning. It means "This is what I am." The thrust of every dream is to tell you something about yourself, your wishes, and your fears.

You don't need to be an expert on Freud and Jung to begin working with dreams and discovering their hidden truths about yourself. You can begin tonight. Don't let the ambiguous nature of dreams lead you to think that they are impossibly obscure. Just like the poem that lures you back to re-read it because of its ambiguous imagery, so do dream images require closer study and greater effort. Ultimately the dream itself will provide the interpretation and meaning, because dreams are products of one's own genius. All you need is the interest to remember and record your dreams, and a willing suspension of disbelief to accept the dream images on their own terms as reflections of some aspect of your soul. Remember, it is not just Walt Whitman who contains multitudes. It is you.

EXERCISE:

Day Dreams

This exercise is not about daydreaming, but it will help you take the images of your nightly dreams into your waking life and keep them with you during the day. There are several easy and fun ways to do this.

Draw or paint the dream. If you can't put the entire dream on one piece of paper, draw the major image or landscape or situation, or make a series of drawings. Then put it in an accessible location so that you can see it and think about it during the day.

If drawing is not your forte, simply give the dream a title. You might write several variations of the title. How would the title read if it appeared in the *National Enquirer*? In the *Wall Street Journal*? In a children's magazine? You could also write a movie title for it and then create the newspaper or poster ad for the movie.

Condense the theme of the dream into a short poem or haiku, making sure you use at least two of the strongest images of the dream. Then recite the poem to yourself during the day.

Look for synchronicities. If you dreamed of a dead cat, look for one over the next few days. It might be in a magazine or on the sidewalk. If you dreamed about a co-worker or neighbor, observe that person closely in terms of your dream image of him or her. You might even call, write, or tell the person that he or she was in your dream, then tell the dream, asking if it has meaning for that person. You'll be amazed how often it does. Some dreams have a prophetic quality. Some are indeed examples of precognition.

Don't overlook the most obvious connection between your waking life and your dream life. The day's events prior to the dream (or perhaps two or three days prior) are often the material about which we dream. Be ready for distortions and exaggerations. Time, place, and proportion are never the same in a dream as in waking reality. For example, you may have a fight with your boss and then at night dream of fighting off a dragon or Communist invaders or a rabid dog. The events and people of our daily lives creep into dreams fantastically masked and disguised. But look for them, and ask yourself why they became this or that image in your dream.

Lastly, take any image in the dream and assume that it is

some part of yourself. The car is the "car part of me." The house is the "house part of me." The old woman is the "old woman part of me." And so forth. Again, on first glance, the connection with you may not be immediately obvious. But play with it. Keep it in your consciousness for a day or so. Make an effort to observe that side of yourself in your daily round of activities.

It is estimated that the average person spends about seven years of his or her entire life in a dream state. One-third of our lives are spent sleeping, and studies have shown that everyone dreams deeply about once every ninety minutes. Whether it is seven years or seventeen years, the information processed through the mind while in the dream state is important in our quest for self-understanding. The images that come, no matter how frightful or bizarre, are images that our unconscious minds find suitable for whatever issues they are trying to resolve. To ignore those images completely is to deprive yourself of a rich reservoir of self-knowledge where your genius resides. Don't be discouraged if your dreams are filled with ambiguity. Most people's are. And the reason is both simple and obvious: people are ambiguous. People, like life itself, need interpretation and reflection.

Poetic Ambiguity

It's curious that people who don't ordinarily read or write poetry will admit that when they are going through some particularly traumatic experience something urges them to write verse. People who fall in love are prone to poetry. What is it that makes perfectly normal people lapse into poetic flights of fancy? There is a clue in the fact that such people only occasionally admit that they have written poetry and very seldom will they let anyone else read it. It's private. It's for no one's eyes but their own. Why should these folks be closet poets? Is there a muse of poetry who seduces even the hardcore rationalist? Can the scientific worldview be cracked on the right occasion by what Keats and the Romantics called "poesy"? In *A Midsummer Night's Dream,* Shakespeare has Theseus exclaim that "The lunatic, the lover and the poet/ Are of imagination all compact." Do we sense a logical truth in this and not want to admit to being a poet for fear it groups us in the same category as lovers and lunatics?

In spite of the fact that scientists, physicians, statesmen, and business people have all written poetry (and some of them number among the world's great poets), it's true that poetry pulls one into a worldview that is quite similar to that of the lunatic or the lover. It is a worldview where reason and clarity hold little power, where fantasy, "unreality," and ambiguity dominate. The phrase "poetic license" has always been interpreted to mean that the poet is allowed to break the rules of proper grammar, but it means more than that. Poetic license is also the freedom to break the rules of everyday reality, to see things that others don't see, to imagine worlds that others would say do not exist, to pile image upon image until their meanings may be clear only to the poet. Indeed, the writing of verses during times of trauma (and that includes falling in love!) is frequently the means by which a person expresses to herself or himself feelings, thoughts, fears, and wishes that no one else can understand. Some of these feelings may be unclear even to the poet at the time. For the poet does not need an acceptable reason for every phrase. It feels right to the poet. It says what the poet wants to say, and that's reason enough.

A direct way to tap into your genius is to begin writing poetry. But for now let's just use poetry as a way of immersing our minds, both left and right brain, into poetic ambiguity. The following exercise lets the two halves of the brain play tug of war with poetic ambiguity. It won't matter which side wins, because what usually happens is that both halves end up running in the same direction, pulled into the rich pool of poetry where ambiguity reigns, where things are not as they seem and where truth becomes a powerful and comforting hunch.

<u>EXERCISE:</u>

Beats Me!

Beat poetry works best. Allen Ginsberg, Lawrence Ferlinghetti, Jack Kerouac, and other mid-century American poets influenced by the Beat movement wrote poems that irritated the more traditional poets precisely because of their obscurity. The Beats conjoined ideas and images, wedded metaphors to realities in new and startling ways so that the "meaning" of the poem was often not apparent on the first reading. Sometimes not even on the tenth reading.

But you don't have to use Beat poetry; surrealist and symbolist poetry is also rich in ambiguity, as are many of the more traditional poems of the nineteenth century Romantics. Consider phrases such as these from Rimbaud: "I live seated, like an angel in the hands of a barber" and "I have carefully swallowed my dreams." Or Whitman's live oak tree in Louisiana that was "uttering joyous leaves." Ferlinghetti's "Coney Island of the Mind." Even Robert Frost, considered an "easy" poet by many people, turned phrases that can keep you surprised for a long time: "essence of winter sleep is on the night" and "slave to a springtime passion for the earth."

So, find a poet whose work is sufficiently rich in metaphor and ambiguity and select any phrase or line that particularly excites you or arouses your curiosity. Then work with it as you worked with dream images or the images given you by your partner in "I See You" or the images and metaphors you used for spontaneous divination. Write them out, place them somewhere where you will see them at odd moments during the day. Put them in your journal. Submit the key words in the phrase to hurricane thinking. Meditate on them. You might even ask a friend or colleague what the phrase means to him or her.

The result of working and playing with ambiguous lines from a poem is similar to what happens to a Zen monk trying to crack the meaning of a koan or Zen riddle. While there may be no perfect answer, nevertheless, while the mind is engaged with the images and metaphors, something wonderful happens. The monks call it satori or enlightenment. You might call it insight. What I meant by the two halves of your brain giving up the tug of war and joining forces is that after wrestling for all the possible meanings, sifting through interpretations or applications, and trying to understand what the poet may have originally had in mind, you will discover that neither side of the brain has to win. The left side will feel good having discovered some meanings. The right half will delight in knowing, on an intuitive level, that other meanings exist which may never be articulated by the left side. A sort of friendship with your phrase will develop. You'll feel at ease with it, like you do with a good friend, knowing that there are things you understand about the friend and yet resigned to the fact that there will always be some part you will never know. A good poem is like a friend. It can comfort, support, stay with you, give advice, and help you sort out your life. On occasion it will aggravate you! But it will always live independently of you, never completely caught in the categories of your individual mind, never your slave. And like a friend, the poem will change over the years. You, the poems, and the times are always shifting and realigning, discovering new aspects of yourselves, presenting new contexts in which to be understood.

The voice of doubt will learn to live with ambiguity. Your genius understands at a flash what it means to be like a tree "uttering joyous leaves." It has sounded the "essence of winter sleep upon the night." It understands the feeling of being "an angel in the hands of a barber." It even identifies with the barber! Doubt may keep trying to destroy your imaginative perceptions of reality, but it will fail. You will learn that all of doubt's objections about the certainty of this or that create the challenge that genius hopes for. "Are you sure?" queries doubt. And genius answers joyously, "NO!"

Now let's write poetry. But let's not try to write any long or highly stylized poems. We will forget about form, meter, and rhyme. All of that's too easy. Instead we will write very short phrases, but difficult ones. Worse, we're going to find those phrases in the streets and alleys where we live.

EXERCISE:

Inscaping

Gerard Manley Hopkins coined a word, "inscape," to refer to a quality he noticed in physical reality and which has kept Hopkins scholars arguing ever since. Precisely what Hopkins meant may never be fully understood by anyone but himself. But it seems that for Hopkins inscape was a combination of three things, shape or form, sensory detail, and feeling. When the inscape of a scene or view struck him, he created some marvelously descriptive and provocative phrases. A sky filled up with "great bulks of brassy cloud." A mountain range became a "theater of thorny peaks." He saw "foam-cuffs in the river." The sky was a "confused pale green and blue with faint horned rays." At other times he felt "soft pulses of light." And a line in his diary reads simply, "Moonlight hanging or dropping on treetops like blue cobwebs." How easily these phrases came to Hopkins we may never know. For our purposes, however, we will learn to construct them step by step.

First, when writing an inscape phrase, select ambiguous

words, that is, words that can be interpreted in several ways. Here are some examples.

For shape or form: square, round, face, roof, hill, strip, fret, ball, slope, bend.

For sensory detail: Brassy, blue, rough, cold, wet, deep, dark, sparkled, enameled.

For feeling: confused, joyful, tired, impatient, worried, fretting.

When you use a word that could refer to either shape, detail, or feeling—or all three—that word will enrich your inscape phrase with more levels of meaning.

Now let's construct an inscape.

As I look out my window at Brooklyn, I see what millions of New Yorkers are confronted with every day: fire escapes. What phrase could be created to express the inscape of a simple image like a fire escape?

First, shape or form. Several possibilities present themselves, but let's say "slope." Fire escapes slope.

Second, sensory detail. Iron.

Third, feeling. What emotions are associated with or expressed by fire escapes? Impatience is one.

So having inscaped the fire escape, we get the phrase "impatient slope of iron." Variations are "iron slope of impatience" and "impatient iron slope."

It may not be worthy of a Hopkins poem, but it serves our purposes quite well. Now that I have it, what will I do with it? Well, I could just sit and think about it for a while. But since I wrote this one deductively, that is, I looked at the fire escape first and then created the phrase, the next step should be to keep it in mind over the next few days and see if I can discover scenes other than fire escapes that embody the same inscape. Perhaps a bridge or a building under construction.

Or you can try a variation on this exercise. Do it inductively: without any particular scene or object in mind, create a threefold phrase that makes some kind of sense (be easy on yourself at the start!) and then go looking for it. For example, how about a "tired rusty face" or the "tired face of rust"? Spend an afternoon scouting around your neighborhood and search for a scene or object to match this phrase or one of your own. To show how easy this one is, I just looked out my window and found it—a fire escape!

Genius can be heard when the voice of doubt is silenced. There are easy and effective ways to silence doubt. You've learned a few of them in this chapter. However you apply them, keep in mind why and how they work. Very simply, they force the mind into new categories of thought. They present the mind with ambiguities that are not easily understood at first glance. They encourage the mind to refrain from viewing the world in polarized terms or creating dichotomies that are mutually exclusive. Creativity and insight occur when you take the risk of perceiving the world around you in slightly skewed or foggy terms, finding the hidden realities that underlie the commonplace. You must trust genius to make sense of them for you.

5 | A New Sense of Time

At my back I always hear
Time's winged chariot drawing near.

—ANDREW MARVELL

If Marvell had lived at the end of the twentieth century instead of in the seventeenth, he might have written his couplet about the wailing throb of an emergency vehicle's siren. It starts low and distant, approaches with an intense frenzy until it is almost earsplitting, then passes by with whirling red lights, and leaves a silent gulp in the throat as one wonders how much time the victim has left. If you live in a noisy city, you might begin to long for Marvell's Time which approaches on the soft wings of an airborne chariot!

The imagery changes from century to century, but the persistent aspect of time that torments all people is its urgency—its unrelenting drive to overtake you, to cheat you of something, a hope, a dream, some plan for the future. To be alive is to be time-bound. Hours, days, weeks, months, years, decades. I used to think that a person was getting old when he or she could say, "But that was twenty years ago," because there was a time when I couldn't remember anything that happened twenty years ago. Then one day I said it—it

111

just slipped out! I didn't really mean it, of course, but I couldn't deny that was what I said. Then I went through a period when I tried not to say it too often. That period didn't last very long. Now I say it a lot, but I like to think it's because a lot has happened in the last twenty—or thirty— years.

And a lot has. For example, time itself has changed dramatically. The new physics has offered us one dramatic change in the very concept of time, namely, that time—and space—are merely constructs of the human mind. In relativistic physics our commonly accepted notions of time have little bearing. Time and space are merely functions of each other, and on the molecular level they practically cease to exist. In other words, what we think of as time is really a cultural description of external reality. To work in subatomic physics means to abandon traditional Western concepts of time, realizing that they are only elements of language. The modern scientist must invent a new language to describe the microcosmic world that exists beneath the fluid and shifting coordinates we call time and space.

In listening to our genius we also adopt the methodology of the scientist: We abandon the concept of time as we have come to understand it when dealing with the external world. Genius does not live and speak in the external world, but in the internal world of our consciousness where time ceases to exist. The unconscious is a timeless world in which genius operates in flashes of understanding, instantaneous enlightenment, apparently coming out of nowhere, revealing ideas that are as quick-winged as Marvell's chariot. It is not that we cease to believe in the time of clocks and calendars, but that for the purpose of working with genius, we willingly suspend our belief in these constructs. We enter a world of noncausal, nonlinear events where time cannot be measured, counted, or predicated on numbers of minutes, days, months. We enter a place where time is truly relative and defies categories such as past, present, or future. Indeed, at the unconscious level, time defies the sensory data with which we recognize its passing in the external world.

You've experienced the relative and illusive quality of time already, even in the material world that stimulates your senses. For example, consider how time is a function of mood. Remember the lecture that was so boring you thought it would never end. Or consider the enjoyable, exhilarating experiences that seemed to pass in a flash: a conversation that was so engrossing you looked at your watch and discovered it was later than you thought; a social event that seemed to end before it had even begun; a moment of lovemaking that you wished could go on forever, so that time would stand still. Why does it always seem to take so much longer to travel to your vacation destination than to return home?

Our perceptions of time vary by age as well as mood. For children time passes slowly. It takes forever for Christmas and birthdays to arrive, the long summer evenings last forever, and the school year looks interminable when viewed from the first day of September. The common experience of adults is that time hurries by—there's too much to do and not enough time. We are constantly amazed that it's Christmas again, so soon! And finally in old age, which is often thought of as one's second childhood, time reverts to its slow, molasses-like pace. The days drag on, the evenings are long, there are hours to pass, days to fill up without enough excitement or activity.

Time has literally annihilated distance. In fact, to estimate distance in terms of time becomes unreliable now that there are such rapid means of transportation. At one time a journey might have taken six days; now it takes less than six hours. Jules Verne's *Around the World in Eighty Days* seems nostalgic and meandering. Not even the moon is eighty days away, and it gets closer every day.

Consider how your body and mind adjust to different conditions of time. The most common experience of this is jet lag, when your body is functioning in one time zone but is physically present in another. Studies performed on people who work at night when most people sleep show how their biological clocks are reversed. Even your own biological and psychological rhythms can be contorted and thrown out of sync with clock time if you eat, sleep, work and play at times that are different from those your body is conditioned to expect.

All these experiences demonstrate that time is merely a frame of reference, and we can and do change that frame of reference when we engage in certain activities, experience certain moods, or pass through different chronological ages. We can also change the frame of reference when tapping into our genius. In fact, if we did so regularly, we would end up in the same "time zone," as it were, in which genius operates, a zone not rigidly divided into past, present, and future, a zone where time doesn't pass either slowly or quickly, and where time is not measured linearly or progressively. Let's adopt the attitude of the modern physicist who must abandon the dominant cultural concepts of time in order to function in a world of relative particles where clocks actually slow down when in motion. It may seem incredible to imagine clocks—our authorities on time—slowing down when in motion, but they do. It is a reality that must be dealt with if one is to engage in scientific endeavors with the unstable subatomic particles that disintegrate with time into other particles. Similarly we must deal with the reality that genius works in a psychic zone that does not conform to our culturally deter-mined constructs of time. It deals with subconscious parti-cles—images, ideas, perceptions—that have their own way of disintegrating into other images, ideas and perceptions, at a rate of time that is infintesimally swift and immeasurable.

Loosen Time's Restraints

You may be wondering what alternatives we have to our standard linear concept of time. How can we even begin to redefine or remeasure time when, like the air we breathe, time seems to be marching past us at its own clip? Indeed, it is difficult for culturally bound people, as we all are, to imagine other time frames than the one dominant in our own culture. As Westerners, we find it difficult to conceive of nonlinear time. But the failure to recognize other types of time perception is similar to being unable to imagine a geometry system other than Euclidian geometry or a number system other than our decimal system. Perceptions are culturally induced constraints, and to break out of them and incorporate alien perceptions into our worldview is no easy feat.

But we know that not all peoples have perceived time as we do, as duration extending into space where the past is behind us and the future is before us. Primal peoples have experienced time as cyclic rather than linear, as infinitely repeatable rather than a succession of nonrepeatable events. Australian aborigines, for instance, believe in what they call the Dreamtime, which occurred at the mythical creation of their world but continues to occur at the present moment as well and can be re-entered by ritual and ceremony. The Hopi Indians have no terms in their language that refer to time. Furthermore, they have no grammatical constructions to imply a past, present, or future. Everything takes place in the present, or it has not yet "arrived." For many primitive peoples there is no distinction between sacred and profane time. The wondrous sacramental events of creation, the exploits of gods and goddesses, the lives of mythical heroes are not dead and gone for them, but are still going on, and they are constantly re-experienced in dreams, rituals, and sacred liturgies.

Genius has the ability to draw into itself both past and

present and on occasion even bestow glimpses of the future. To listen to genius one must be, if even for a split second, in a timeless realm, relating to one's environment in a nonordinary way. Thought transcends time and place, particularly when it is what we might call a "visionary mode of thought." Those phenomena that occur in nonordinary states of consciousness do not fit easily into the confines of linear time. For example, in a dream you may be in one location, and then in a flash you are somewhere else. Or morning may instantly become night. Or your dream may recreate in sharp and accurate detail an event that happened when you were a small child living a thousand miles away. Dream events are real phenomena, but take on an air of unreality because time and place are so unstable in the dream world. If we can temporarily suspend our Western notions and accept a nonlinear, nonphysical time and space, those dream events are no less real.

The exercises in this chapter are designed to loosen our concept of time, pry it out of Western categories, so that we can experience the timeless realm where genius speaks. It won't be one hundred percent successful, because we live in a world where standard and accepted notions of time prevail and indeed must be honored if we are to live in a workable society. But our experiments in dealing with this world through nonordinary constructs of time will help us open up the voice of genius. If we can successfully discover a new time reality, we will be better able to tap into our genius when we need it.

If you have been practicing the exercises so far, you're already more than halfway there. Many of the techniques you've learned so far have loosened your concept of time. Visualization of past and future events, counting your age backward to recall childhood events, searching for synchronicities in waking life, even the exercises to blend contrasting categories are attempts to place consciousness into an eternal present where such distinctions no longer apply. If you've enjoyed these moments it's because the desire to experience an eternal present is perfectly human and natural.

The following exercises will startle your imagination into recognizing that other time zones exist even around you at this moment; they will silence the voice of time that speaks solely in Western concepts; and they will draw past, present, and future into an eternal present.

Rezoning

In 1983 the state of Alaska contracted its four time zones into two. The Aleutian Islands that had formerly been in the Bering Sea time zone are now in the Alaska time zone, which is an hour earlier than the Yukon time zone. The Bering Sea time zone no longer exists in the state of Alaska. Poof! Were it only that easy to manipulate time and discover new time zones! As reported in *The New York Times,* "In the past, the two-hour time difference (between Juneau and Anchorage) meant that Anchorage residents with business in Juneau in the morning had to travel the day before and spend the night in Juneau. Now, when airline schedules become adjusted, they may be able to make the round trip in a day." Again, time and technology annihilate distance. Two cities that were formerly perceived as a day apart in travel time are now closer together. Yet people will undoubtedly adjust to the new time and find themselves just as late as ever. Time's urgency is not alleviated by resetting clocks and redrawing zones on maps. Were the White Rabbit an Alaskan White Rabbit, he'd still be "late, late for a very important date."

EXERCISE:

Time Zones

Here's a curious exercise, guaranteed to create your own unorganized state of wonderland. What get's curiouser and curiouser about it is that the drastic version is easier to cope with than the simpler version.

The Drastic Version: Before going to bed tonight, set your watch five or six hours ahead. Figure out where in the world a time zone matches the time on your watch. It might be London, Moscow, or Hong Kong. Maybe Des Moines, Iowa. Then as the day proceeds, let your watch startle you out of the zone you happen to live in. Each time you look at your watch, say, "Time is relative," and recall that there are real people operating according to the time on your watch, eating lunch while you get dressed, going home from work when you go to lunch, hitting the sack when you "clock out" of the office. Actually, you won't have to repeat the affirmation too often. It will be obvious to you.

The Simple Version: Watch out! This one is dangerous. Set your watch only a half hour or one hour ahead. Worse, set it back. Surprisingly, you will find this more difficult than the drastic version, because it is closer to your actual time. Now, instead of visualizing people making love in London when you look at your watch, you'll think, "I'm late!" And you might be.

The Gutsy Alternative: Don't wear your watch at all. Rely totally on your genius to stay on time. Ask people on the street, catch glimpses of other watches, use the clocks on the wall, listen to the radio or church bells. You might start this exercise on a weekend when you have fewer deadlines. But if you stick with it for a while, you'll probably learn to function rather well without your personal timepiece strapped to your arm like a manacle.

Yes, you may have to explain to people what you're up to, especially those who try to glance furtively at *your* watch. Some won't understand. But all day you will feel as if you are truly in another time zone, not necessarily the one you've set your watch for, but in a kind of special zone that no one but you is aware of. It is a little secret just between you and your genius, to be startled each time you glance at your watch into remembering that you have an experiment going that will free you from time and remind you that genius is with you. Without the assistance of the mis-set watch, you would not have remembered genius. But you are now alert—and maybe late—but keenly aware that time is relative and your genius is with you in the present.

A Time for All Seasons

A major manifestation of time that modern urbanites frequently overlook is seasonal time. When people lived more intimately with nature and their jobs and social activities revolved around the weather and the seasons, cyclic time was paramount and obvious. Today most jobs are not dependent on weather, animals, or natural seasons, and we live in environments that artificially regulate temperature and time and light so we hardly take note of the seasons. For example, there is always that sudden shock on the first evening off daylight savings time as we crawl out of our offices to discover it's already dark. We notice leaves returning gently to trees in springtime and exploding into riotous colors in autumn; we pause at the first snowfall of winter. But these moments of awareness pass too quickly, and we proceed with business as usual, scarcely giving nature a second thought.

And yet seasonal time is a reality that is probably structured into our very genetic make-up, indelibly woven into us over generations of evolution. For instance, there are more murders when the moon is full. Health and comfort suggest we put on a few more pounds in winter and cut our hair shorter in summer. Some primitive urge lures us to lie in the new grass each spring and take off our shoes when we're at a beach in summer—to be on the earth and experience it sensuously. It is easier to wake up and get out of bed in the summer than in the dead of winter (hence the phrase!). These and many vestiges of mood and behavior seem hold over from earlier, more ancient times. We molt, hibernate, fur up, get frisky, shed weight, fall in love, go crazy at rather predictable times of the year. In truth we are still seasonal creatures, no matter how our artificial environment stymies our perceptions of sun and moon, wind and wave, rain and clear skies. Something won't let us get the bountiful play of nature out of our system—not completely.

Genius keeps it there. Our individual genius intersects with the collective genius of everyone, a "still point" where memories of our original condition are stored, memories of when the yearly seasons and the daily weather determined our perceptions of time. In primal terms, the sacred time or Dreamtime still occurs. It has never ceased. The vestiges of seasonal time still lurk beneath the surface of consciousness. If we can nurture an awareness of them, we more fully express our humanness, which is inexorably rooted in the natural world by virtue of our physical bodies and by genetic memories bequeathed by our ancestors.

The following two exercises will stir up those memories and personalize the collective images and symbols with your unique stamp. They will also let you use seasonal images to discover new insights into problem solving and decision making.

EXERCISE:

Seasonal Time

Reflect for a moment on a question you want to ask, a problem you need to solve or a decision that confronts you. If nothing is pressing, do the exercise to endow the day ahead with a unique seasonal quality.

Consider which of the four seasons reflects your mood or state of mind regarding the question, problem, or tasks of the coming day. One will probably call out for your attention. If no season seems related to your present moment, select one by lot. It's possible that any or all of the four seasons will have some relation to your present condition, and so working with any one of them will prove profitable.

You might also use a holiday or festival such as Valentine's Day, Halloween, Thanksgiving, harvest, summer vacation, spring planting. The point is to focus intently on some period or activity directly related to seasonal changes.

Then perform hurricane thinking on the season you have chosen. Using the images and associations that emerge, look for patterns, images, or series of images that shed light on your question or problem. You may get an outright solution or discover considerations that are important to your ultimate decision.

The working mechanism behind this exercise is similar to ones we've used before. It is another method of creating or finding images to invoke our imaginations to do their best work. Genius requires images with their many levels of meaning, their sensory detail, their half-conscious associations in order to fire the synapses of creativity. Without nonordinary imagery and ideas, our thinking is stuck in the ordinary ruts and directions that are no different from day to day. Using imagery that changes with the seasons keeps our awareness freshly loaded with the seeds of new ideas.

EXERCISE:

Astrolomical Time

It's a new word: astrolomical. You won't find it in the dictionary. Let's use it to join two separate but related fields, astronomy and astrology. Neither field by itself may be complete or satisfying enough from your perspective. Astronomy may be too scientific, astrology too bizarre, but both can be luminous vantage points for incorporating new time images into our lives—moons, stars, planets, the sky. Whether you consider the physical effects that heavenly bodies have upon us, such as daylight, nighttime, the tides, moonlight, or their influences on mood and character, the heavens are a rich pool of ever-changing phenomena through which we can tap into our genius.

First, get in the habit of reading the cosmic forecasts in the daily newspaper. Check the time of sunrise, sunset, moonrise, and moonset. The sun is a natural measure of passing time that changes with the seasons while your own daily work schedule remains the same. Just as being aware of other time zones around the globe releases your thinking from being locked in only one zone, so too will your awareness of the setting and rising sun give you a fresh and alternative perspective of the day. Twice a year you will pass through the equinoxes, when day and night are of equal length; twice a year you'll encounter the solstices, when day and night are at their longest or shortest. Some people's moods and creative energies coincide with these cosmic events.

Second, become aware of the phases of the moon. Again, many people report that their energy and interests reflect the changing phases of the moon. For example, spotting the young, virginal sliver of a new moon in the west may influence the observer with a sense of new beginnings, of starting over, of possible futures. A full moon fills the sky and the mind with the image of completion, achievement, and success. In its third phase, the moon wanes, seems to die, shrivel up, retreat, go into seclusion, contract, decline. The virgin, the mother, the crone. Many women find it easy and natural to relate to these cycles because the moon is a traditionally feminine symbol and can represent the physical and psychological changes of the monthly cycle with which it keeps pace. Among American Indians, a woman menstruating was said to be in "her moon lodge."

Third, if you live near the ocean, use the rising and falling tides as alternative measures of time. Pause in the afternoon or late evening or whenever the tide changes. Use that moment to suggest your own changes or reversals. Mark the twenty-four-hour cycle by high and low tides and see if being aware of them gives you a different appreciation of time.

Fourth, learn about the zodiac signs, the mythical characters and creatures that divide the year into twelve parts. You need not adopt a belief in their having determined your life or character, but you can use them as alternative metaphors for the months. Become familiar with their imagery, their myths, their characteristics and personalities. Use them as material for meditation, spontaneous divination, hurricane thinking, or synchronicities. If you use the sun's position in the sky to determine the zodiac sign you'll get a change every month, but using a "witches' calendar," you can trace the moon's path through the twelve sun signs. The moon spends about two days in each sign, so there is frequent turnover. An alternative to zodiac signs is to use various American Indian designations for months: Moon of Frost in the Lodge, Moon of Ripe Berries, Moon When the Grass Returns, and so forth. Different tribes had different aspects to mark the moons, depending on the climate and seasonal changes in which they lived. You can even coin your own: Moon When School Lets Out, Moon When Heating Bills Skyrocket, Moon When Window Screens Go In.

The point is to give each month or week or day a character and personality of its own, making each unique so that one day is not like the next and each Monday not like every other Monday. There was a wisdom in the medieval church that created the calendar of saints' feast days and seasonal holydays to break up the drab round of weeks and months with color, pageantry, and story. For our purposes any system that creates variety and stimulates the imagination will provide a backdrop for tapping into genius.

The Timeless Moment

The artist seeks to capture a moment, freeze it in time and thus defy the inexorable sweep of change and ultimately death itself. Monet's gardens are preserved on canvas as they looked a hundred years ago. Frost's New England is still as fresh and accessible to us at the end of the twentieth century as it was to him in 1900. Dickens's London slums still reek of poverty, garbage, and misery. Every work of art captures a moment and preserves it. In your own life there are moments worthy of artistic preservation, even though they are not spectacular excursions into love and romance or traumatic retreats into sorrow and pity. After all, some of the world's greatest poems and paintings capture the most ordinary moments, the most lackluster events. The following exercise is designed to create "still points" of time in your own life by freezing them in a simple yet challenging form of poetry, the haiku.

EXERCISE:

The Hidden Haiku

The great haiku poets achieved a remarkable tension in their short, three-line verses. The tension is between two images, one expressing change, instability, transience, impermanence; the other expressing the unchanging, stable, permanent, eternal quality of the event. This contrast, poised precariously between two images in only seventeen syllables, is what strikes us as an almost perfect haiku.

Some examples:

> An old silent pond . . .
> into the pond a frog jumps,
> plop! Silence again.
> —Basho

> Even I who have
> no lover . . . I love this time
> of new kimonos.
> —Onitsura

When the autumn wind
scatters peonies, a few
petals fall in pairs.
                              —Buson

If you reflect on your own life, even just the past day, you will recognize moments when an ongoing, changeless state of existence contrasted sharply with a momentary, shifting event. At such a moment you realize instinctively that you dwell in at least two dimensions of time. In everyone's life there is the silent ancient pond and the transient plop of a jumping frog, the long sorrow of having no lover and the festival of wearing new kimonos. At such moments past, present, and future meet in a kind of still point in which you see several layers of meaning and existence.

To use haiku in your own life as doorways into another sense of time, you can simply begin by reading them frequently. They are short and can be read as inspirational verses before retiring at night or on rising in the morning. Meditate on one or write about it in your journal, or elaborate on the two contrasting images with the hurricane technique. Use it as an affirmation during the day or look for parallels between the event in the poem and the events of your own day.

Eventually write your own. Instead of summing up the day in a single metaphor or lengthy paragraphs of journal entries, write a haiku. It doesn't have to be a great poem. You can even fudge on the seventeen syllables if need be. Simply look for a moment in the day when you experienced the tension between the timeless and the ephemeral, where the linear progressive event intersected with the eternal moment. You might even write a haiku about a problem you are attempting to solve or a decision you need to make, whether it be about sending a critical memo at work or planning a birthday party for your children. You'll find that in working with contrasting images you'll see how various options juxtapose themselves and reveal their consistencies or inconsistencies.

Aerobic Time

If you regularly engage in some type of aerobic exercise, such as swimming, jogging, dancing, or brisk walking, you can transform those minutes or hours into an exercise in timelessness. As we have seen in the exercise "Enchanted Chanting," any constantly repeated word, phrase, or sound will lift the mind into a light trance state, similar to the hypnagogic state between waking and sleep where your sense of time is less acute. Whether the mind is dancing—bobbing along on a word or sound—or your body is dancing—along a running track or across a swimming pool—the resultant state of timelessness is as therapeutic to your consciousness as the physical activity is to your body. However you achieve this light trance, you open the channels for communicating with genius. When you are lifted out of the time-space framework you normally operate within and become slightly mesmerized by an activity or sound, you create a state of readiness to hear genius. Do this intentionally and regularly so that you look forward to the timeless quality of your exercise as well as the physical purpose of it.

There are other, less strenuous ways to achieve this mesmerized condition. We've looked at some already. Focus on a candle in a dim room, repeat a sound or word over and over, watch the smoke curl from incense, observe the trickle of rain down a window pane. Or go outdoors and stare at clouds, listen to the wind, watch the movement across the surface of water, fix your consciousness on the pounding surf. However you choose, the goal is to quell your consciousness of time and experience the timelessness that is present even in the changing scene around you.

The Nonlinear Diary

The book we use for a diary or journal is a system of linear information par excellence. It consists of lines of words, sequential pages, numbered in perfect order, the days of the year lined up in progression from January 1 to December 31. The book itself is finite, with a front and a back, and the pages become compartmentalized by months, weeks, and days. There is no avoiding the linear quality of a diary or journal. But how to temper it? How to take the events of your life that appear to occur in sequence and break that sequence? As those events sink into memory, they will not stay in any particular order, nor will your genius recall them for you in right order. Order matters little to genius. In fact, to reshuffle those events provides new insights into them, new sequences and juxtapositions that may induce you to question how you feel and think about them.

EXERCISE:

The Main Event

This is a method of recording the events of a single day. You can use your regular diary or journal. At the close of day, select the most significant or unusual event that transpired during the day and place it at the top of the page, and free associate from it with the other events of the day. After you've covered all the activities and happenings you care to, write about them in that new order, addressing the question of why they came back to you in that particular order.

EXERCISE:

Week in Review

Your left brain will like this. Choose some scheme for organizing the week's major events. Sort out the adventures and misadventures by categories. You can use ordinary categories, such as athletic, cultural, career, family, happy, sad, successes, failures.

Or use nonordinary, metaphorical categories, such as escapes, entrapments, dragons slayed, clouds broken through, deserts crossed, births and deaths. Use as few or as many categories as you choose. Use contrasting opposites or ones that are rather similar. Lift the ordinary events of your week out of the ordinary time and place categories so you can view them differently.

EXERCISE:

A Month of Sundays

Buy a spiral notebook of at least thirty pages. Each day, open at random and record your thoughts, events, impressions of the day. Jump around in the book from day to day so that your days are out of sequence. At the end of the month, read through them from start to finish. Observing the last thirty days of your life out of sequence allows you to evaluate the events from a different perspective.

Whether time sneaks up on you in a winged chariot or with a voice blaring like an ambulance siren, the effect is the same: to seduce you into believing that events march forward in unique and unrepeatable fashion. "The past is past, the future has not arrived, so live for the moment." Sound advice? Partially. Indeed, we should live in the present moment. But is the past past? Is the future still ahead? Only in linear terms. From the vantage point of genius, or in the timeless regions of the unconscious, all time—past and future—is here now. Now is the day of creativity. How many inventive ideas have been squelched by a voice that warned, "The time's not ripe for that" or "Give up. There's not enough time." Ignore that voice. Listen to genius.

6 | See the World Twice

How wondrous! How mysterious!
I carry fuel, I draw water!

—ZEN APHORISM

Whether we carry fuel, draw water, write manuscripts, sell vegetables, design greeting cards, fill out income tax forms, teach children, manage an office, or simply work in one, we often fail to notice the mystery and wonder in the activities we perform. We are caught in the routine performance of duties that blinds us to the meaning behind those duties. We imagine real meaning is somewhere else, perhaps in the world outside, passing us by. And so we long to break our daily routine and enter that world beyond the work environment where we spend so many hours of the day. Yet in wishing to do so, we miss two worlds: We miss the outside world that we imagine to be more carefree and spontaneous, and we miss the world revolving around us as close as the very tasks in which we are engaged. The Zen aphorism above is a call to notice that world of humble ordinary tasks and witness the spark of genius that is in them. Wondrous to carry logs inside for the furnace, you ask? Mysterious to turn on the cold water faucet, you wonder? Yes!—but to see the mystery and wonder, we must be able to look at the world twice.

The Native American writer Jamake Highwater was once berated by an old medicine man for being too preoccupied with words. But after all, thought Highwater, words are how I make my living—writing, reading, teaching. Why not be preoccupied with words? The old man explained to him:

> You must learn to look at the world twice. First you must bring your eyes together in front so you can see each droplet of rain on the grass, so you can see the smoke rising from an anthill in the sunshine. *Nothing* should escape your notice. But you must learn to look again, with your eyes at the very edge of what is visible. Now you must see dimly if you wish to see things that are dim—visions, mist, and cloud-people . . . animals which hurry past you in the dark. You must learn to look at the world twice if you wish to see all that there is to see.

Have you ever asked someone to enumerate the businesses, shops, signboards, and various other things he or she passes on the way to work each day? Many people can't number more than four or five. And yet they see them every day, even gaze at them for periods of time as they wait for a red light. It is easy to move through our daily world oblivious to what is right before our eyes. We don't look twice.

Furthermore, we fail to look beyond "the very edge of what is visible" where we could see how mysterious, how wondrous the parts of our daily world are. We fail to see the world as myth, drama, and metaphor, we miss the value of things, we find our minds rebuffed by the barricade of material reality. We suppose the blank surface of things is all there is, as if no human drama were taking place behind the half-pulled curtain across the street, as if no one suffered inside the hospital we drive past, as if someone's skill and craft did not go into creating the billboard that makes us smile each morning on the way to work. Seeing beyond the edge of what is visible, on one level, means looking for the human or spiritual element beyond, behind, and beneath physical reality.

On another level, seeing beyond the edge of things means looking within ourselves, where meaning, value, understanding, appreciation, and sympathy with other creatures reside. If we are too preoccupied with the daily cares of making a living for ourselves and our families, we find little time to gaze into ourselves where wondrous fuel is carried and thirsts are quenched with mysterious waters. We resist entering that interior realm where genius communicates.

The demands of our daily routine can easily prevent us from meeting our emotional and personal responsibilities to those we love. They keep us isolated from family and friends. They keep us from really getting to know ourselves. With such little time, we stop nurturing our growth, cultivating the life of the spirit, listening to our genius.

If you have been doing the exercises presented so far, the effort to find time to practice the exercises has already disrupted your normal routine and broken daily habits to some extent. Nevertheless, it is easy to fall back into the habit of seeing no further dimension to daily chores than their drudgery, their sameness, their blandness. Drawing water is merely drawing water. Writing a memo is merely writing a memo. Filling a gas tank is merely filling a gas tank. It is easy to stop looking at the edge of things. When you feel yourself slip back into the ordinary way of performing your daily chores, you might need some new inspiration. Here is an exercise to relocate your attention to the edge of things. It is a useful strategy to clear your mind for a half hour when you've reached a mental block over some assignment at work or when you need to come up with a fresh idea to impress your supervisor.

EXERCISE:

The Edge of Things

This exercise has a visual version and a mental version. First, the visual method.

Contour Line Drawing: This is looking at the edge of things with a vengeance. In her handbook, *Drawing on the Right Side of the Brain*, Betty Edwards explains the method of contour drawing. In brief, it goes like this: Pick an object such as a chair, vase, lamp, your hand, the window, whatever. Then tape a blank piece of drawing paper to a table. Sit at the table with a pencil so that your body and face are turned away from the paper and focused on the model you intend to draw. Before you begin drawing, look long and hard at the edge of the object. Let your eyes roam along its edges, noticing the contours, the different shapes. You might even consider the space around the object as being a complimentary opposite contour to the one you will draw.

When you are sufficiently familiar with the object's edge, begin to draw it as slowly as possible on the paper without taking your eyes off the object. Do not look at your drawing until you are completely finished. Keep your eye on the edge of the object and move along it very slowly, moving your hand equally slowly. Keeping your hand and eye in pace with each other is crucial. It may take half an hour or more to draw a simple object with infintesimal movements of the eye and hand, but you will be surprised how accurately you have drawn the object when you are through.

The Mental Method: Select a poem of at least thirty lines, but no more than sixty lines, and spend a half hour reading it. Set a timer. Just read one poem repeatedly for a half hour. You may end up having it memorized, and that's fine; it then becomes a rich deposit of images and ideas in your mental reservoir. But something else should happen to you as you read the poem slowly and repeatedly for a length of time, stopping now and then to consider some image or reflect on the meaning of a line. You will begin to see beyond the edge of the content of the poem. Trees, mountains, people, cities, buckets, apples, night, fears—all the images of the poem will, as the old medicine man told Highwater, "grow dim" and you'll see the people behind them, the animals, and the spirit or energy that they acquire because they are in a poem and are now moving into your consciousness.

In addition to helping you see beyond the edge of things and forcing you into looking at things twice, this exercise will slow you down. If you intend to seriously break the habits and routines of your daily life, you must slow down, physically and mentally. Doctors recommend that we slow down physically because it reduces stress. In addition, it helps to slow down with creative activities such as these precisely because they are not part of your daily routine. So slow down, look sharp, look more than once. See what there is to see.

Mastery Versus Mystery

As human technology has gained more mastery over the physical environment, we have lost our sense of the mystery of that environment. An archetypal moment in the history of this shift from mystery to mastery was when Ben Franklin stuck a lightning rod on top of his house. God-fearing people all over the country soon realized that they did not have to worry about God striking their house with lightning during a storm as punishment for their sins. Western technology has come a long way since Ben flew his kite and performed his other experiments; and the average human being now has incredible mastery over the immediate environment. It has been a mixed blessing, as we know, for in its wake the new technology has brought its own kind of punishment and pollution for Mother Earth.

On a personal scale, we each like routine because it is an expression of our mastery over our little corner of the world. We know exactly where the toothpaste is. We alone know how to tease the feisty windshield wiper on our car to make it work. In dozens of little ways throughout the day we exert control over our physical lives, if not always over our psychological lives, where moods, emotions, and feelings have a way of wriggling out of our grasp. They don't hearken to our commands so readily. Our emotions, our inner fears, even our joys can be like the cloud-people who keep shifting shape or like the animals that rush past us in the dark. But the toothpaste, at least, stays put.

We need an alternative perception of the world as a place where we are *not* in control, where we share our place with other creatures, where the nonhuman have power and knowledge to teach us. Often when we need to come up with a new idea, we are blocked precisely because all our ideas come from our "master mind" and eventually we exhaust those ideas. We need to find alternative ideas that come from some other source than our mastery. If we willingly adopt a sense of kinship with all created life, we can see value, meaning, and insight in other creatures. We are then on more intimate terms with other beings both visible and invisible. We learn to stop when the cat stops and looks up into the air, seeing or sensing some presence invisible to us. Eventually we see what spooked the cat.

Lame Deer, a Sioux religious leader, tells us how the Indian mode of seeing things can turn ordinary daily tasks such as boiling water into spiritual, kinship experiences.

I'm an Indian. I think about ordinary, common things like this pot. The bubbling water comes from the rain cloud. It represents the sky. The fire comes from the sun which warms us all— men, animals, trees. The meat stands for the four-legged creatures, our animal brothers, who gave of themselves so that we should live. The steam becomes a cloud again. These things are sacred. Looking at the pot full of good soup, I am thinking how, in this simple manner, Wakan Tanka takes care of me. We Sioux spend a lot of time thinking about everyday things, which in our mind are mixed up with the spiritual. We see in the world around us many symbols that teach us the meaning of life. We have a saying that the white man sees so little, he must see with only one eye. We see a lot that you no longer notice. You could notice if you wanted to, but you are usually too busy. We Indians live in a world of symbols and images where the spiritual and the commonplace are one. To you symbols are just words, spoken or written in a book. To us they are part of nature, part of ourselves—the earth, the sun, the wind and the rain, stones, trees, animals, even little insects like ants and grasshoppers. We try to understand them not with the head but with the heart, and we need no more than a hint to give us the meaning.

At some point we need to reclaim our sense of the sacredness of all life. We need to recognize that all plant and animal life has some important contribution to make both to life on earth and to the life of our minds. Primal people believed in the divinity of animals with rights, feelings, sensibilities, even powers greater than humans'. We have lost that belief in the modern assumption that we are more highly evolved than animals.

The archetypal psychologist James Hillman points out that in ancient times the more autonomous an animal was, the more humans were inclined to treat the animal as some kind of god. Snakes, insects, wolves, and other fiercely independent creatures expressed an almost godlike defiance of human efforts to tame them, so ancient people revered them. Today, we fear them. We still sense their specialness, their "otherness." They are not like the animals we admit into our homes, the ones we tame, control, transform into domestic beings like ourselves, thus reducing that otherness.

Birds have always had a particular fascination for human beings. Even in the age of flight, we admire their ability to soar through the air with a disarming effortlessness. It is a feat that will most likely continue to astound us, at least until technology equips us with individual wing-packs or flight-chips or some such contraption. Flight has always represented freedom and transcendence, two experiences that have an eternal appeal to the human spirit. We all crave freedom in some form or another. We all desire to transcend our own circumstances, even if it means merely staying home from work for a day or getting our minds unstuck when we need to tap into our genius on the spur of the moment. We would all like to be better, more godlike, more supernatural. Flight is the perfect metaphor for both freedom and transcendence.

EXERCISE:

We Are All Relatives

Certain Native American tribes end many ceremonies with the phrase "We are all relatives." By this is meant not just the "two-leggeds" who participated in the ceremony but all "four-leggeds," rocks, plants, even the elusive cloud-people! In whatever ways we can incorporate this worldview into our own lives, we temper the arrogance of mastery we exercise over external reality. We temper our feelings of being in control. We begin to perceive ourselves in relation to other created things, sharing the environment with regard for one another. We boil water and find it wondrous and mysterious. We begin to draw new ideas and insights from a nonhuman environment and apply them to the human.

Several previous exercises, such as "I See You," "Beats Me," and "Inscaping," used animals, plants, landscapes, and other natural images for tapping into your genius. Think back and rediscover the animal images that meant something special for you. Keep those images in your consciousness and reflect on ways that you are like them, and they like you. You may already have a kind of animal totem that you collect—owls, whales, pigs, penguins, teddy bears. These are animal spirits that already permeate your consciousness and perhaps your home. They have knowledge and wisdom to teach you. You already feel drawn to them for some reason. Read up on them, and learn as much as you can.

In these and any other ways you have discovered, disrupt your daily routine and defy the voice of habit. Genius is ready to offer fresh ideas and bold new concepts but is thwarted by a life that is too comfortable, too complacent, too predictable.

The Daily Routine

In little ways throughout the day you can break the comfortable and predictable way you order your activities. Any little rupture in routine helps to silence the voice of habit. Merely walking down the other side of the street you usually walk may give you visual perceptions you never noticed before. Take a different route to work or home. Leave five minutes earlier and take a brief walk around the park before heading for the office. See what it looks like at 7:30 in the morning! Try shopping in a different grocery store, perhaps in a different neighborhood. Get dressed backwards, reversing the usual order in which you put on the first, second, and third item. You may actually forget one!

A difficult strategy for many people but one of the best for freeing your mind is to "prodianate," a new word Webster hasn't discovered yet. It means the opposite of procrastinate. It's not easy to prodianate, to do today instead of put off for tomorrow some unpleasant chore. But it is a way of breaking up today's routine, and it loosens up tomorrow's schedule as well. Willingly choose to perform some undesirable task today, right now, and get it over with. In the long run you'll have more free time for goofing off and hanging out with your genius.

Your Stuff

Have you ever noticed how much of your day is taken up with taking care of your stuff? Your clothes, your car, your house, your yard, your pets, your books, your records, your games, your hobbies. We each have a collection of material possessions, unlike any other's collection, that makes our lives unique. Living in a comfortable consumer society as we do, it's almost impossible to live simply and reduce the number of things we own. Buying and owning is a way of life, yet it is a practice that has been criticized throughout the ages as being inimical to the life of the spirit, the life of genius. As Thoreau said, "Simplify, simplify, simplify." And yet few of us can go out to a cabin by a pond and live a bare, spartan existence like he did—few of us would want to! But we are faced with a challenge regarding our material possessions. They can dominate our daily lives. They cement the routine of our days and weeks together. If we want to change that routine, we've got to learn ways to get along without too much preoccupation—physical and mental—with our stuff.

We all know the caricature of the staunch materialist who flatly denies any reality that he or she can't see, feel, kick, or punch. A curious irony is that genuine poverty also has the same power to trap the mind in material things. As many a revolutionary has discovered throughout history, the starving masses care little about idealistic slogans such as liberty, equality, and fraternity. They want food, shelter, and clothing. They want jobs. So we have a strangely disturbing polarity: Obsession with material things is found both among those who own many things and center their lives around them and among the very poor who lack the necessities and dedicate their lives to acquiring them. Getting and taking care of material possessions can so preoccupy the mind that the life of the mind suffers. Thoreau raised the provocative question about whether the farmer owned the farm or the farm owned the farmer who could never get away from it.

Perhaps that is why the ideal that has inspired many people is "poverty in spirit." Being poor in spirit or nonattached to possessions frees the mind and heart to pursue the higher ideals of genius.

In *A Separate Reality,* Don Juan instructed Carlos Castaneda in the virtue of "controlled folly." Consider everything, he said, to be unimportant, equal, and meaningless. Then decide what you will *choose* to be important. And begin treating only those things with concern and passion. It is not easy to practice "controlled folly," but it is a way of eliminating unnecessary preoccupation with your possessions.

Some people actually define themselves by what they own. Their sense of identity is rooted in particular clothes, cars, houses, memberships, books they've read, awards they've won. If you suggest to them that they do without one thing or another, you touch sensitive nerves. For you are not merely telling them to forget about this or that thing, you are asking them to excise part of their personality, to cut a portion of their self-identity out of their psyches. It is like dismemberment. Let's try it.

EXERCISE:

Dismemberment

This exercise uses the same strategy as "Stripping Down to the Essential You" explained in Chapter 3. This time, write on ten strips of paper ten material possessions that are to some extent or other bound to your self-concept, things that help you define yourself both to yourself and to others. If you don't feel that you define your identity in terms of material things, then just list ten favorite possessions that you would find it hard to live without. Stack them in order of importance, the most important going on the bottom. Proceed as in the Stripping Down exercise and see how it affects you. Consider what would happen if you had to eliminate each possession from your life. Who would you be without it? This process will jolt your consciousness with the possibility that the essential you may not be woven so tightly into material things.

Most of us have wondered at some point in our lives what we would want to have with us were we shipwrecked on a desert island: what food, what books, what objects, and most of all what companion. It's a fun fantasy, but relatively safe because none of us really know what we would be like on a desert island. Berserk, most likely! So let's make this fantasy more realistic.

EXERCISE:

Doing Without

Use your standard visualization technique to spend fifteen or twenty minutes visualizing your life without one of your most important possessions. The car is one obvious start. Then try the TV, phone, radio, books, pets. Do one at a time. Be inventive. How would you function without this particular item? What emergency survival strategies would you employ? What substitutes could you find? Visualize your feelings about life without the item as well as the physical activities that would be stunted or thwarted without it.

If you have the nerve to test yourself, create a little adversity for yourself now. Actually do without something for a day, an evening, a weekend, or entire week. Leave the car at home and take public transportation. Spend a week without watching TV. Fast for a day. Don't read anything over the weekend. You may decide life is hell without these things. But you will at least have gone on a modified "vision quest," a period of self-imposed deprivation when you need to rely upon your genius. And genius will seldom fail you in such situations.

The Awesome Environment

It is no coincidence that many people get their best ideas while walking along a beach, listening to a pounding surf, camping out under a starry sky, or sitting on a mountaintop overlooking a deep lush valley. These are awesome environments, and they have the power to trigger extraordinary thoughts. Almost anything opposite to our normal everyday experiences can serve as a cue for genius to speak.

Ancient people had a belief and trust in mysterious awe-inspiring places to transmit the voices of the gods to them—places that literally take the breath away, or mesmerize, like crashing waves, wind in the trees, mist or steam spiraling up from a fissure in the earth. Anyone who has walked from a busy city street into the hushed grandeur of a Gothic cathedral has experienced this same sense of otherworldliness. Retreating to natural spots—call them your "power spots"—can give the necessary solitude and appropriate physical stimulation to hear genius. An awesome environment can tune the mind into eternity, putting it in touch with the truth and wisdom that lies within one.

Thoreau liked to consider the possibility that some ponds were bottomless. Even though he would probably have never found one had he plumbed the depths of every pond in New England, he would still have argued that it is good for humankind to keep believing in bottomless ponds. It is an example of "controlled folly"—believing *as if* some ponds are bottomless. Why? Because in some mysterious way we measure our own depths by the depths of natural phenomena. When you look into a pond or a canyon or into the light years of outerspace, you are really measuring the depths of your own nature. Thoreau asked, "What if all ponds were shallow? Would it not react on the minds of men? I am thankful that this pond was made deep and pure for a symbol. While men believe in the infinite some ponds will be thought to be bottomless."

This is a basic truth about the relationship between the human mind and the universe: in order to keep faith in the infinite possibilities of the human mind, we need to have faith in the immensity and awesomeness of the universe itself. The two reinforce and nurture each other. We and the world we live in are not as distinct and opposed as we may sometimes think. It does us well, therefore, to go out regularly into the natural world, to seek out some awesome place where the magnitude or beauty or power of nature overwhelms us.

7

Away from the Crowd

The world . . . is stupendous, awesome, mysterious, unfathomable; my interest has been to convince you that you must assume responsibility for being here, in this marvelous world, in this marvelous desert, in this marvelous time.

—CARLOS CASTANEDA

Imagine what would happen if Los Angeles were completely smogfree, and one dark night while everyone was sleeping, smog suddenly appeared. The next morning hundreds of thousands of terrified people would probably run for their lives into the mountains to escape the "beast" that had invaded the metropolitan area. The reason why no one flees now is that the smog crept in gradually over several generations so that residents hardly noticed it. Now people consider it normal.

Imagine what would happen if there had never been stars in the sky, and one (very) dark night while people were sleeping, they appeared. And a lonely insomniac noticed them. The next morning he told everyone to stay up that night and look at the sky. Emerson considered this possibility and concluded that people would probably fall down on their knees and adore and believe in the beauty above them. The reason why no one falls down to worship stars today is that we have grown used to them. They are always there. They are normal.

How is it that we can become oblivious to stars and smog, two phenomena that should take our breath away, in one way or another? The answer is simple: Familiarity breeds forgetfulness, if not contempt, and thus we take much of what we live with, both beautiful and beastly, for granted. The facts of our daily existence can become almost invisible to our conscious awareness because we live on such intimate terms with them.

The same is true of genius. You may have been struck by a curious paradox. The exercises for listening to your genius that seemed rather unusual at first most likely revealed insights, ideas, and feelings that, on second glance, were not all that strange—for you. They seemed at once alien and unique, yet oddly normal, oddly *yours*. Ironically, when we delve into the deepest parts of our psyches, we discover a reality that we instinctively know has been with us for a long time, waiting to surface. As we discovered in our journey back into childhood, we reclaimed visions, hopes, and dreams that had been lying dormant. Genius is like that. It may take innovative strategies to wake it up, demand restructuring parts of one's daily life, require drastic stretches of one's ordinary imagination to detect its voice, but when genius speaks, the message has the ring of something very old, very ancient, almost forgotten, but never quite lost. Like the smog in Los Angeles and the stars overhead, genius is near, yet we often fail to recognize its influence on us. We ignore its power as one of the primary ordering principles in our lives. Instead, we surrender to the crowd.

Most of us let the voice of the crowd drown out the voice of genius. We assume the ordinary ideas and echo the uninspired statements of the majority of human beings. We slip into mediocre patterns of thought, believe only in the same assumptions that everyone agrees upon. In the final analysis, we become no different from anyone else—same thoughts, visions, hopes, ideas, perceptions, and attitudes. Then we wonder why we never come up with challenging ideas or bold new concepts or alternative solutions to our own personal problems and those of society at large. Not only do we continue to reinvent the wheel and rediscover fire, we compliment ourselves for doing so! But when those compliments wear thin, as they always do, when genius taps us on the shoulder and asks, "Is that the best you can do?" we feel weak, foolish, and often powerless. We begin to envy the great men and women of the ages and imagine that only they possessed genius, that only they could take charge of their lives and channel creative energies into projects that made a significant impact.

It is easy to grow oblivious to the personal power that is our genius. We don't recognize it or experience it because we won't let ourselves deviate from the crowd. We choose to remain blind to what makes each of us "genuine," what makes us "ingenius," as the Romans said. In Latin "ingenius" means "innate abilities," the talents and insights we were born with, the feelings and desires we can't eliminate no matter how adept we are at ignoring them. The vital power locked in our original nature accompanies us from birth, perhaps even before birth, and will be with us far into the future. Such power should not go untapped. And yet in most people it does.

Original intuitive energy can be threatening, both to ourselves and others. The crowd is frightened of genius because when people hear the voice of genius uttered by someone else they recognize their own neglected thoughts. Being unique and speaking with the voice of genius, you confront others with their own tarnished uniqueness, reminding them that they refuse to draw on their own personal sources of wisdom and courage. As you dare to live according to your genius, it becomes less threatening to you, but others, less experienced with genius, still perceive the threat.

Psychologists have written much in recent years about

becoming self-motivated and inner-directed, rather than other-directed. In their own distinctive jargon they have advised: Discover you genius, your own personal source of meaning and value, and live by it. It's truly awesome to us to choose to be directed by an inner force over which the rational and culturally conditioned ego has so little control. But those people who have made the choice attest to the freedom they enjoy when they rely on the voice of genius. They experience an independence of thought and action. They become self-reliant, trusting their own resources, searching within themselves for answers and insights to problems the crowd considers too hopeless to solve. No problem is too complex, no circumstances too defeating, if you listen to genius.

To live confidently with genius means getting over the fear of failure. We have all failed at something in our lives, most of us many times. To stand on one's own genius, to defy the crowd and to take whatever comes, may appear to be courting failure, but in the long run, if we are true to ourselves, we cannot fail. Fear of failure is really the fear of being different, of being out of step with others, of espousing ideas, visions, and values not shared by the majority. But why fear that? Each of us *is* different! In spite of the accepted mores of modern life and the many common traits that all humans share, each of us has a unique inner core, a heart of pure genius that speaks from the collective wisdom of the universe without diminishing our individuality.

If we are not committed to being directed by our genius, we are trapped into letting others direct us, letting the crowd dictate how to live, what to think, what to value, what to love, and what to hate. To survive the crowd means to live creatively, whether it be developing new ideas for a career, discovering innovative ways to strengthen a marriage, devising strategies to raise children, or finding effective methods of curbing the destructive forces of politics and technology that threaten all life on earth. To survive in any situation means taking responsibility for your personal life. Choose to be responsible and live according to the principle of "controlled folly," where *you* decide what is important and valuable. Genuine and ingenius individuals throughout history have taken the responsibility for maintaining their own interior reality, "keeping their spirits alive," as it were; as a result they have exerted profound influence on external events as well. They listened to their genius and shaped the world in which they lived. You too can follow their examples—and their insights—for being independent of the crowd does not mean rejecting the wisdom of the ages.

There are times when confronting the crowd requires physical and psychic retreat—getting off on your own, taking time to be by yourself, seeking out solitary places. As you know from doing the exercises in this book, to tap into your genius often means being alone. Like an ally, genius needs attention. The alliance must be nourished and strengthened by time together. Any quiet time alone without distractions can help silence the competing voices. Reflecting on the day's events, recording thoughts, wishes, or fears in a journal, relaxing in your room, altering your usual routines, visiting an awesome environment—all of these are invitations to genius.

Every creative person attests to the importance of solitude. It is not a luxury but an absolute necessity for nurturing the life of the spirit and mind. The distractions of ordinary life can overwhelm the creative spirit even as they stimulate it. Every stimulating experience needs a period of incubation, time to reflect, to consider options, to let the excitement of inspiration swell up in you and carry you forward on its crest. To be effectively creative requires keeping the crowd in its place—always within reach, but sometimes at a distance compatible with the silent territory where genius leads you to communicate with the human spirit as it takes shape and form in *you* individually.

Genius can speak to everyone. It has spoken to you. You've heard it, felt it, implemented its advice. You have opened yourself up to the wisdom and knowledge that only it can give you. Each time we hear the voice of genius, we are reminded that the strategies and mental gymnastics we employ to tap into it are merely preparation, training, conditioning in awareness. At best we can only practice at expanding our consciousness, faithfully perform our psychic workouts, put ourselves on alert, and let the creative ideas gestate within us until they are ready to be born. In their own good time they will leap forth passionately and unexpectedly. The best ideas and noblest visions always appear with a life of their own, waiting to be grasped by those who are committed to excellence and have conditioned themselves for the task. As we prepare ourselves to hear genius, it speaks from the deepest sources of our personal being like some driving energy that was always available to us, but of which we were unaware. Often an exuberance of joy and energy springs from having recognized that in the process of tapping into our genius we have tapped into something larger, deeper, and more powerful than ourselves—for the thoughts and feelings that are most uniquely our own are merely on loan to us. They are ours for only a time, to use, to enjoy, to serve, but their own hidden sources lie in a genius that transcends each of us individually. They belong—as do we—to the collective genius of the universe.

8 | Speaking with the Voice of Genius

The strategies for thinking, feeling, and living creatively that you have learned can prepare you to speak with the voice of your own genius on any occasion. Armed with insights and perspectives that are unique to you and different from the crowd, you can solve very practical problems—in *your* way, not in the ways the crowd has been trying to solve similar problems and failing. Every challenge is personal and requires your own personal response. Let's think back over some of these strategies and see how they function as power bases from which you can tackle any problem and confront any challenge whether large or small.

Troubling Situations

In "Your Mind's Eye" you learned visualization techniques that enable you to rehearse troubling situations that you must face. As in "Inventing Your Behavior," you can use visualization as a pre-game warmup before an important meeting with a supervisor in which you want to suggest a change in your job responsibilities or in the way certain policies are being carried out in your department. You can try out different arguments, visualize his or her reactions to them, and most of all see yourself maintaining your cool composure no matter how the supervisor responds.

Not only can you visualize what you will say, but you can "feel" how you will feel and practice responses for the possible ways the other will feel and react. You'll feel more self-assured, more ready to handle unexpected turns of events. In the process of previewing for yourself every possible detail of the situation, you will discover which strategies, words, or responses stand the best chance of achieving what you want.

Stating Your Case

You have learned several exercises that will strengthen your skills in using symbols and metaphors, a crucial strategy in winning arguments, explaining your position, defending an idea, proving your point. "Proper Symbol," "Deepening the Metaphor," and "Single Metaphor" show you how to come up with the perfect analogy to elucidate how you feel about something or someone. A strong, clear analogy is often the deciding factor in opening up other's eyes, in helping them to see things your way, or simply in unblocking their minds so that they too can contribute fresh ideas to the problem you are trying to resolve together.

For example, you might be involved in a personal relationship that is taking up too much of your time, but you don't want to break it off altogether; you simply need more space to nurture your private life. Stating your case with a convincing metaphor about growth or one that suggests the relationship will acquire a stronger bond like Kahlil Gibran's metaphor about the need for space between two pillars that support a magnificent temple, may provide insight that helps your friend understand your position and agree with you. It may even help you understand the relationship better.

Discovering New Options

We've seen how categorical thinking can be the bane of creative problem solving. Trapped into always perceiving situations in the same categorical terms, we find it difficult to break out of them. One category that can restrict thinking so that we never resolve issues is the category of the self. In seeing things from only one point of view, we are doomed to recycle our same worn-out ideas. "Hurricane Thinking," "Janus Blitz," and "Search and List" can be applied at the start of any enterprise in which you want to break loose from constricting categories, whether the undertaking be stressful, like asking for a raise or a promotion, or suggesting to co-workers or family members that you should do things differently, or pleasant, like trying to determine how to spend extra money. Saturate yourself with as many options and alternatives as you can discover, then select the ones that will be the most effective or successful.

In deciding vacation plans, for instance, you may be stuck in the same old category of what you think is appropriate for summer holidays, such as going to a beach to lie in the sun and swim. But if you "blitz" over the goals you'd like to achieve on your vacation, you might discover that less strenuous activities are what you really need—time alone or with a friend, time to read or to take long walks away from the city environment. You might realize that a restful two weeks in a cabin in the mountains is what your life needs most this year, and so you won't park yourself on the same beach as you usually do.

Don't forget to seek advice from others. "I See You" is an excellent game to gather ideas from a friend or companion, not in terms of what you should decide, but in terms of how you are deciding. When your partner tells you how he or she perceives you acting and thinking in a given situation, you derive greater insight into the ways you usually respond.

Reacting Emotionally

One of the most ingenious methods of solving problems and making tough decisions is to pick up clues that apply to the situation from wherever they may be hiding—within you or without. Being able to read your emotions accurately is a good place to begin, and exercises such as "Recording Your Unexpressed Emotions" and "Flicking Your Emotional Shutter" will get you started. When you develop a reliable perspective on your emotional life (not the same as controlling your emotions!), you'll be able to anticipate the feelings that can determine your thinking and behavior, and when necessary, disregard them or attempt to respond from an alternative emotional base.

Parents, for example, may find that they always react emotionally to their teenagers' rebellious escapades in the same way—either holding back how they really feel or over-reacting when the misbehavior is not very serious. Each incident is unique and calls for a parent to thoroughly trust his or her emotional reactions, and what's even harder, to know how forcefully to release those emotions. Getting to know your own emotional reactions requires thoughtful consideration at quiet times when you aren't gripped by the emotion itself.

Clues for Solutions

The more adept you become at reading clues that offer information for the decision-making process, the more innovative and realistic those decisions will be. A simple exercise such as "Pet Rock" will train you to pick up signals from others and from situations themselves. Just as you had to give the rock the benefit of the doubt (on many counts!), so too will you see the value in giving other people the benefit of the doubt when you try to understand their points of view or struggle to see things from their perspective. "Getting in Sync with the Universe" has trained many people to become more alert to the coincidences and synchronicities of situations that are not always immediately apparent. How often has your genius shown you that the best solution or the most successful approach in dealing with some dilemma was always within reach, right under your nose?

So the next time you have a problem with someone, perhaps a neighbor who's always waking you up on weekends with his lawn mower, spend some time seeing the situaton from his point of view before you confront him. Give him the benefit of the doubt, and look for clues to the solution in the way he usually operates. You may discover a very easy way to get him to be more sensitive to your family's needs.

Mulling It Over

Every creative undertaking involves getting away from it for awhile. It's necessary to let ideas incubate, to give your conscious and unconscious mind time to mull things over. "Spontaneous Divination" techniques can move you physically into another space or invite your attention into some other mental environment, both of which can provide the breathing space you may need to reach conclusions. An hour or two in an "Awesome Environment" can't be beat as a refreshing break from problems and worries that just might be blocking their own answers from you by keeping them below the threshold of consciousness. Remember, tapping into your genius almost always involves silencing the distractions around you—even when those distractions are the problems themselves, and ironically, problems usually are their own worse distractions! So get away from them for a while, take a stroll, look out the window, read the comic strip or a poem.

The Right Time Is Now

Genius is timeless, and exercises like "Time Zones" can help you release the voice of genius. How often you've been told (or you've told yourself) that the time is just not ripe for such-and-such an idea. Precisely, and it's usually due to the fact that *you* are not ripe for the idea. Time has a devious way of blocking ideas, of putting mental blinders on our imaginations. Fresh ideas always seem to be ahead of their time, but how often we are surprised to find that the time is ready for them. So get your mind unstuck from clock time as much as you can. Have the courage to express your ideas, but don't take offense if they are not immediately accepted. Others may need time to incubate them too.

At your next business or organization meeting, let down the guard that blocks you from stating your opinions or offering suggestions. Don't hesitate because you think you'll be considered foolish. More often than not the time *is* ripe for considering your ideas. Even if they are not adopted, they may provide the stimulation needed at the moment to move the group forward. "Youthening" will remind you of ingenious moments in your past. Of course, it may recall occasions when you failed to act with genius, but that's okay; we learn from our mistakes. Don't, however, make the mistake of not learning from your successes! Recall past triumphs and victories frequently and continue to learn from them.

Evaluating Values

Most important decisions and programs in your life involve personal values. High or low values motivate each of us in our daily concerns—whether to eat another piece of chocolate cake, to exercise, read a book, call home, buy someone a gift, go to bed early. Exercises like "Making Friends with the Imp" will let you reassess the underlying values that influence your thinking on any given problem, large or small. By adopting opposite values, or discarding your own temporarily to approach a problem from a new perspective, even a "perverse" perspective, you will derive new insights. Think perversely and you may even reconfirm and strengthen your commitment to your old values and realize that they should determine your decision. "Stripping Down to the Essential You" is another way to reconsider the values upon which you tend to base decisions. In "Doing Without" you can assess how you would handle a situation without your normal everyday crutches. It will force you to visualize how you would survive without the material supports on which you usually rely. As is often said, necessity is the mother of invention. How would you entertain your children on a weekend if the TV were on the fritz? What kind of a date could you go on with your car in the shop? How would you spend your vacation if you blew all your savings on dental bills? "Catastrophizing" once in a while, even just in reverie, will unlock alternative strategies that you might want to implement even without the crisis!

Most of these genius exercises are as practical as you make them. Solving problems creatively, arriving at workable solutions, making good decisions always involves an interchange between what is already inside you and what lies without. Living ingeniously requires heightened awareness about yourself and the world around you. As in the "Inscaping" exercise your task is to discern the true shape or form of a problem, then the key detail or details, and the motivational impulses within you that influence the overall situation. The more practice you have at expanding your awareness, seeing possibilities, divining solutions, the more easily you'll be able to speak with the voice of genius.

You *can* speak with the voice of genius. You've heard it, felt it, implemented its advice. It has spoken to you.